And Poison Fell From the Sky

Also from Islandport Press

Mountain Girl
Marilyn Moss Rockefeller

Moon in Full
Marpheen Chann

The Ghosts of Walter Crockett
W. Edward Crockett

Dear Maine
Morgan Rielly and Reza Jalali

Take It Easy
John Duncan

Whatever It Takes
May Davidson

Nine Mile Bridge
Helen Hamlin

Hauling by Hand
Dean Lawrence Lunt

Available at www.islandportpress.com

And Poison Fell From the Sky

A Memoir of Life, Death, and Survival
in Maine's Cancer Valley

Marie Thérèse Martin

ISLANDPORT PRESS

ISLANDPORT PRESS

Islandport Press
P.O. Box 10
Yarmouth, Maine 04096
www.islandportpress.com
info@islandportpress.com

ISBN: 978-1-952143-39-7
Ebook ISBN: 978-1-952143-61-8
Library of Congress Control Number: 2022932036

Printed in the United States of America
All photographs, unless noted, courtesy of MarieThérèse Martin.

Dean L. Lunt | Editor-in-Chief, Publisher
Piper K. Wilber | Assistant Editor
Ron Currie, Jr. | Editor-at-Large
Dylan Andrews | Book Designer
Emily A. Lunt | Book & Cover Designer
Cover image by Cappi Thompson | Getty Images
Editorial by Rex Roades (p. 157-158) | Maine Today Media

To those who find themselves in abusive spousal relationships
with nowhere to go,
and
for those who suffer the consequences of industrial toxic
chemical exposure and injury without understanding or warning
or both.

Table of Contents

Foreword

Rumford and Mexico, Maine, like many towns in America, were once small tourist destinations, capitalizing on healing mineral springs and access to the great outdoors. The area boasted a few nice hotels, theaters, social clubs, churches, and sports teams. Rumford and Mexico were not unlike the imaginary town Rachel Carson wrote of in the opening lines of her 1962 book *Silent Spring*: "There was once a town in the heart of America where all life seemed to be in harmony with its surroundings." But in the end, Carson's town, like Rumford and Mexico, was a place that seemed to live quietly and safely while, in truth, it had not. In fact, this is the nut of MarieThérèse "Terry" Martin's memoir, *And Poison Fell from the Sky*.

Terry is a storyteller, born from other storytellers of Acadian heritage. While their homeland may have vanished in the Acadian genocide in 1755, their stories and trauma remain in Terry's blood and echo in the landscapes of her life. Terry was a small-town Catholic girl with big-city dreams that were foiled by powers beyond what she felt she could control, which is probably similar to how Acadians felt when leaving France in the 1600s and how they felt when leaving Canada for New England to work in its industrial mills. Rachel Carson grasped this in *Silent Spring*: There is always a story behind the story that is hardly ever told. In continuing the description of her imaginary town, Carson said, "Some evil spell had settled on the community . . . Everywhere was the shadow of death . . . There had been several sudden and unexplained deaths, not only among the adults but also among the children."

As a young mother and nurse, Terry witnessed a similar "evil spell," which she writes about here. And in her text, she has taken back what was taken from her years ago—her story—about being on the front lines between industry and disease but also on the front lines of abuse—in her state, in her town, in her church, in her role as a nursing student, in her home. In writing about her first day of nursing orientation, where she witnessed a woman being given electroshock therapy, Terry writes, "I would do what I had done before: store the memory of these events in a dark corner of my mind, write about it in my journal, and deal with it at a later time."

With this book, she no longer has to live in the shadow of any of these things. In America, the fundamental need for bodies to be respected has always been at odds with the goals of industry. History has shown these abuses to be true, from medieval dike builders in the Loire Valley to the paper mills of rural Maine. Terry followed those circuitous routes and ended up, surprisingly, whole. Why? Her DNA is of strong stuff, made from ancestors whom Colonel Winslow tried to snuff out in 1755. But they survived, and so did she.

Genetics do not explain everything about who we are. Identity is more complex. It's made of social, cultural, and environmental legacies and can be harmed by others who do not have your best interests in mind. Terry took (to use a line from her text) "notes both sound and sour" from her life and spun them to mend the fractures in her heart. I think she will help others do the same. She helped me. I depended on her story, her ideas, and her friendship for ten years while working on my own book, *Mill Town*, about these same two towns. And while Terry tells me she is proud of my tenacity, without her I wouldn't have had the courage to write what I did.

Terry's wisdom, compassion, and fortitude are evident in every word she writes. It feels like she is telling you stories sitting by a fireplace on a cold snowy night—intimate, warm, with a little magic and often some humor. Which, by the way, happened one night at my house over a few glasses of wine. It wasn't the wine or the fire that made her go from tentative to dynamic storyteller; it was what came from depths that most of us will never reach.

—Kerri Arsenault
Roxbury, Connecticut
March 2022

Prologue

A Revelation

On an inescapable hot and humid night in the early 1970s, the air felt so thick in my bedroom that it was hard to breathe. Even though I shut and locked the windows in our drafty old house, pungent odors from the nearby Rumford paper mill always managed to work their way inside. The rotten-egg smell seemed particularly strong in the wee hours of quiet summer nights along the polluted Androscoggin River. But it was just a bad smell, right? The smell of money, the mill bosses always told us.

Suddenly, Edward "Doc" Martin, my husband, sat bolt upright in our bed, sweat dripping from his forehead.

"What's the matter?" I asked, still half asleep, but fearing an urgent problem, either personal or with a patient.

Doc and I, physician and registered nurse, operated a family medical practice in an office attached to our house. It was somewhat quaint and our regular patients usually had stories to tell—pretty typical in a small community in the seventies. But increasingly it seemed their stories were about cancer: who had it, who might have it, who died, and maybe details about the next fundraiser to help a cancer family in need. Doc, although a man

1

with dark secrets who could be terrifying behind closed doors, was also a remarkably compassionate professional and a relentlessly curious soul. It bothered him and he couldn't figure it all out—until now.

"Water, air, chemicals, unregulated dumping, cancer, disease—they are all connected!" he blurted out.

"What?" I responded.

We didn't fall back to sleep. We talked until the sun rose over what, just a few years later, the media would dub "Cancer Valley." Doc's middle-of-the-night revelation would forever change and, at times, nearly destroy our lives. The issue and the debate eventually prompted one of the most famous cancer hospitals in the world to call Doc and ask him straight out: "What the hell's going on in Rumford?"

For me and my hometown, the answer to *that* question was a long and painful journey.

This is my story.

And Poison
Fell From
the Sky

One

Everything Changes

I still remember the exact day in my life when everything changed. I was ten years old, and I would never feel safe again. This day started out as any other at our home on Knox Street. My mother stood at the electric stove wearing a bibbed apron as she made dinner for her family. My father sat in his red vinyl reclining chair reading the daily newspaper, as some fathers did, waiting for supper to be served promptly at five, as he had plans for the evening.

"Hey Van, what's for dinner tonight?" he shouted to my mother from the next room.

Evangeline was my mother's name. She was named after the heroine of the Henry Wadsworth Longfellow poem of the same name. Ironically, the poem is much better known today than the event Longfellow wrote to commemorate—the Acadian Deportation, when thousands of my family's people were forcibly removed from their homes in Canada by the British. Mother stood at only five-foot-two, but her name carried huge significance.

"Pot roast," she answered brightly.

She fixed dinner using a copper-bottomed set of pots and pans, a wedding gift from twelve years earlier. The aroma of her pot roast filled the house, and to this day, whenever I smell a pot roast, I am transported back to that afternoon. My brother, Rick, and sister, Andrea, were each in their rooms reading, and I was standing at an old wooden ironing board, hot iron in hand, carefully pressing my mother's nursing uniforms to perfection. I took the job seriously, dreaming that someday I, too, would become a nurse and wear a starched white uniform.

The radio played a countdown of popular songs sung by such stars as Patti Page and Nat King Cole. This was the scene that day. Everything peaceful, everyone seemingly happy. None of us—not even my father—had any idea what was about to happen, that all of our lives would be suddenly and forever upended.

To me, my family—mom, dad, two siblings, and I—seemed like any traditional and typical American family in the 1950s. My dad, Arthur, could be described as Lincolnesque in stature. He was tall and walked with a gentle stoop, giving him a vulnerable look. He worked as an undertaker and ran the film projector at the local movie theater. He was usually home for supper, which was great, but the rest of the time, he was gone. He seemed wrapped up in his own little world—hardly a part of ours. He seemed uninterested in family life, meaning he seldom engaged with his roles as a husband or as a father. Like the blank square on a Scrabble board, he had the promise of unused potential.

Mother, who worked as a nurses' aid, was the complete opposite. She came from a loving family and was prepared to duplicate what she had been taught as a child into adulthood. As a loving

My family and me in the fifties in Rumford. In the back row is me, my mother, and my father. In the front are my sister Andrea and brother Rick.

mother and a dutiful wife, she had convinced herself she was living in a happy marriage.

In the 1950s, Rumford had a population of about ten thousand people (by 2020 it dropped to less than six thousand). The town, located on the Androscoggin River and in the foothills of the White Mountains, was settled in 1782 and incorporated in 1800. Most importantly for what it became, Rumford was located at the site of Pennacook Falls where the Androscoggin drops an amazing 177 feet over solid granite. Mexico, a smaller town but still very much a "mill town," was located across the river. Mexico had a population of 4,762 in 1950.

Rumford lived a sleepy existance for roughly its first one hundred years. In 1882, Hugh J. Chisholm recognized the massive pontential of the Pennacook Falls for making paper. Chisholm purchased more than one thousand acres of land. He built the Portland and Rumford Falls Railway to connect Rumford to the national rail network in 1892. He also established the Rumford Falls Power Company in 1890. He soon opened the first paper mill, which eventually became the Oxford Paper Company in 1901. People flocked to the town for work, and it grew from a population of 898 in 1890 to 3,770 just ten years later, and finally to 10,340 by 1930. At the direction of Chisholm, much of the town's housing was built during the early part of the century, including Strathglass Park, built specifically for employee housing. It was added to the National Register of Historic Places in 1974. The entrance to the oval-shaped, tree-lined development was marked by a granite gateway. The Oxford Paper Company paid for the maintentance. It also invested in the community center as well as schools, hospitals, and churches.

In its first few years, the mill became the sole producer of postcards for the US Postal Service and by the 1930s was known for the quality of its coated papers for magazines and books. Chisholm also established International Paper. Business was booming.

By the time I was a child growing up in town, that paper mill seemed an enormous, timeless presence. In the sixties it would employ more than three thousand people. The mill towered above us, casting a shadow over the entire town. Yes, the process of making paper smelled bad, but we lived on top of a hill, which allowed us to avoid some of it. We would defend the offensive odors to visiting cousins, saying it "wasn't that bad," though it was. And yes, the mill made a lot of noise. It was tough falling asleep at night to the sounds of a paper mill moaning and groaning like an old man, while trains screeched as they stopped and started over and over and over again. Staying asleep was impossible.

It seemed to me that the mill ran continuously every day and every night during my entire childhood. I could see the stacks from my house and the mill was just *always* going. As it hummed and cranked, the noises became the familiar sound of my generation and stood as a backdrop to every important event of my young life. This very large industrial center—we called it the Kingdom of Paper—sprawled in all directions. As demand for paper increased, the demand for everything used in that process also increased. This papermaking industry stood immovable, and the mill's presence was a constant reminder of its power. It would have been hard for me to imagine, back then, that the mill could ever become a bigger aspect of my life. In the years to come, it would do just that, looming even larger, until it dominated everything.

When I was a child, the mill had one rival in any effort to achieve complete dominance over Rumford—the Catholic Church. I attended a local parochial school through eighth grade. There were two parishes in my town that were separated from each other by only one street, but the true distance between them seemed much greater. One was a French-speaking Catholic Church, and the other was English-speaking and identified as Irish Catholic. Once while visiting Prince Edward Island, the place my grandparents came from, we stopped at the cemetery, looking for ancestors, and discovered the exact same division even among the dead. French Catholics were buried on one side and Irish Catholics on the other. Little had changed since those days. My grandmother cried for days when one of her sons announced that he would be married in the Irish Catholic Church by an Irish priest. She remained inconsolable, and we kids remained confused. Our generation didn't feel the ethnic divide as starkly as our parents and grandparents did. Like the mill, the Church would play a major role in my life.

On that fateful day on Knox Street when I was ten, as my mother cooked her pot roast and as I ironed and as my siblings read and as my father waited for dinner, we heard a knock on the back door. It was a quiet, gentle sound, almost as though the person knocking wished to apologize for doing so.

My brother opened the door, exchanged a few words with the visitor, then turned back toward the kitchen.

"Mom, a lady wants you," he announced in his most important seven-year-old voice. Somehow, instinctively, he knew something important was about to happen.

We turned our heads in unison, looking across the kitchen to the back door.

My father recognized the uninvited guest immediately. He panicked.

"Oh shit!" he said.

"What's wrong, Art?" my mother asked, watching the color disappear from his face.

He said nothing. He hurried into the bathroom and locked the door behind him.

Bemused, she went to the back door. On the other side of the screen stood a middle-aged woman with gray hair and sad, tired eyes. She wore black stubby heels and was wrapped in a heavy dark cardigan. She had walked nearly three miles in those shoes, climbing one of the biggest hills in town, to arrive at our home during the dinner hour to deliver her message.

After a brief conversation, Mother walked back into the house, suddenly looking just as sad and tired as the mystery woman. She attempted to talk to my father, but he stayed locked in the bathroom. When he finally came out, she'd had enough time to gather herself, get over her shock, and now was just angry.

"Is this true?" she demanded.

It was.

My father was having an affair with a young woman, and her mother had walked up the hill to tell my mother personally.

In reality, he was cheating on all of us. We would all suffer fallout from his faithlessness. I would never call him Dad again.

This was not the first time he had dishonored his marriage vows, but it would be the last. My mother was fresh out of forgiveness and would not make or hear any further excuses.

She emptied every closet and drawer, tossing everything he owned into one big pile on the back porch. My siblings and I spent the night alone in our rooms, trying to make sense of all this, trying to understand what our lives would become without him around.

What we did know was that our father was gone—leaving behind three young children, a wife, and a dog. Our mother was in her room, quietly crying. The pot roast burned slowly in the oven.

Early the next morning before leaving for work, my mother gathered the three of us in a straight line and said, "If your father comes back today, don't let him in."

No one responded.

"Do you understand me?" she asked sharply.

We nodded rapidly.

We understood, but what a demand to make of three kids! My sister, who was five years old, appointed herself as guardian of the back door. She was already showing signs of a fiesty and independent spirit. But while her personality bordered on being difficult, her decisions, even at that young age, were thoughtful and reflected her feelings in the moment.

Father did come back, as Mother predicted, and asked Sissy to open the door. He wanted the television set.

"You can't come in," she said. "Momma said not to let you in."

She was resolved to mind her mother and to keep the only thing that mattered to her in that father–daughter relationship— a small black-and-white television set.

"Let me in," he said, "or I won't be your daddy anymore."

After a short pause, she looked him straight in the eye and said, "That's okay. I would rather have the television set."

Two

Don't Breathe

Divorce made us all pariahs. Two years went by, with spotty financial support from our father, although he still lived in town, and our mother struggled to be the primary breadwinner of our fractured family. She worked one full-time job at the hospital as a nurses' aid and another full-time job guiding us toward adulthood. On many nights, I heard her cry. A thin wall separated our bedrooms, and as often as not, the sound of her weeping was my lullaby.

And it wasn't just the pressures of supporting and raising three kids on her own. She still loved my dad, and she would feel his absence throughout the rest of her life. We all did. Even though he was a detached father, the house still seemed more hollow with him gone, loss echoing in every room. Our traditional family became untraditional as a family of divorce, numbered four instead of five, and everything changed.

Our father had functioned like a cardboard cutout of a smiling movie star that could be moved from one room to the next. He was seldom around and was emotionally unavailable all of the time. Even though it was bad with him there part-time, things felt worse in his absence. His presence reminded me of an occasional guest that you look forward to seeing but are never really sure why. As three young children holding out hope that we would be a whole family again, his final departure signalled the loss of that hope.

Through it all, I tried to keep busy. On most Saturday mornings, my best friend Katherine and I walked to downtown Rumford. We tried to avoid breathing fumes from the paper mill by turning our walk into a game we called, "Don't Breathe." When one of us caught the rotten-egg smell in the air, we'd yell, "Don't breathe!" and the two of us would run, holding our breath, until we thought we'd gone far enough that the air had cleared. With an experimental sniff, if the smell was gone, we'd say, "All clear."

It was fun, and we giggled our way downtown, playacting exaggerated distress whenever the smell hit our noses. But we also knew, I think, that it wasn't really a game. If we took a deep breath, the caustic fumes made our chests burn. On some level, we realized that breathing the mill exhaust wasn't good for us, so we found a way to protect ourselves by making it into a game.

We'd spend the day window-shopping, sharing school stories, and buying lunch with the allowance we'd earned that week. Sitting at the Woolworths counter, we bought food and pretended we were adults. Usually, we ordered hot dogs and a Cokes. As we grew into our teens, the freedom of those Saturday morning excursions helped us develop our emerging personalities. With little cultural stimulation in our town, display windows of retail shops were like museums to me. I especially liked the jewelry store windows with their gold and silver pieces and fine collections of colorful glass and Limoges china. I could hardly wait from one week to the next to see the newest additions.

On one of those Saturday mornings, I arrived at Katherine's house earlier than normal. I could hear Katherine and her mother arguing—about me.

"Find another friend, Kathy!" her mother yelled. "I don't want you hanging around kids whose parents are divorced! No good will come of it!"

I held my breath, frozen in place on the grimy garage floor. I felt guilty for something I hadn't chosen and did not want. I knew we had the dubious distinction of being a rare family of divorce in town. The Catholic Church didn't recognize divorce; it was considered a sin. But how was I—or my mother or my brother and sister—guilty? My father was responsible for all of it. He made the choice to stray from his marriage. Nevertheless, it was obvious that Katherine's mother—and probably others—saw the stain of sin on my whole family.

At twelve, I didn't have any answers. I just knew it felt lousy.

Katherine rushed out of the house, pushing the screen door open and nearly knocking me over.

"Come on, let's get out of here!" she said.

We left for our usual Saturday morning adventure, and after Katherine calmed down, it was like the fight with her mother never happened. She never mentioned anything about it, but it was easier for her to forget her mother's judgment than for me.

The Rumford-Mexico area had its own class system, and like it or not, Katherine and I were on different rungs of the ladder. She had two parents. I didn't. Her dad owned a business and had political clout in the town. Mine didn't. Although her dad didn't work at the paper mill, as an undertaker he depended on the benefits of papermaking to run his business. Most everyone did in one way or another. He reverently placed corpses in burial plots once the spark of life had disappeared. He dressed withered bodies, plumping them up with a composite to disguise the depletion of tissues ravaged by illness. He was a kind of miracle worker, resurrecting loved ones with rouge, lipstick, and a fresh shampoo. He could make you forget that someone was dead, and if you forgot that, you didn't ask uncomfortable questions about how, or why, they died. Finally, he buried the evidence in cemetery plots blessed by the Catholic priest.

The class system was real and rigid and revolved entirely around the mill. The mill bosses lived in big houses with sprawling lawns that someone else mowed, while the salaried workers bought or built homes in nice neighborhoods near the schools. The salaried workers managed the hourly workers, who were responsible for the actual labor of making paper. Before the advent of job-safety regulations, many of these hourly papermakers worked without shoes. Early photos show men standing in groups, side by each, all barefoot. They lived in tenements on the flat areas near the dirtiest stretch of the Androscoggin River, crammed between the water and the road, not a blade of grass to be seen. Their clothes reeked of the mill, and most workers undressed on the porch before entering the house in an attempt to leave the stink outside.

It didn't work.

Many of the tenements had outside porches where families could sit on good days, when the wind blew particulate matter downriver. They sat with a view of the mill yard, passing the time by shooting rats that foraged for scraps along the banks of the river. Their kids played in the streets with balls and tin cans. These folks seldom complained, accepting what they had and being grateful for it. It helped that they were taught compliance on Sundays, in churches filled with the faithful. Modest as their lives may have been, they were proud of their craft and for their designation as the best papermakers on the East Coast. The opportunities to make the leap from hourly work to salaried were few.

Many early French Canadian immigrants anglicized their names in an attempt to embrace their new lives, adapting to English versions. They turned their backs on their mother tongue, learning English in an attempt to get ahead. For their effort they were teased and laughed at as they stumbled over words that had the wrong meaning or were difficult to pronounce. The nuns were strict disciplinarians and would bloody the knuckles of any child caught speaking French in their classrooms. As grade-schoolers at St. John's School, we were given two choices—speak English or be silent. Without really understanding the implications, we abandoned our own language and history.

On top of the baseline stigma of being French, my family was also marked as one of divorce. Our mother was known as a "grass widow," a derogatory term for a woman whose husband had walked out on her. Judgment was silent but omnipresent and utterly damning.

I didn't know what to do with that judgment and I was embarrassed by it, so I, too, remained quiet.

Three

Number 24

There was never enough time or money. Mother struggled under the weight of looking after three children while working every day caring for patients. Alone with curious, hungry, and energetic kids, she decided to ease her burden by finding someplace else for me to go.

Near the end of my eighth-grade year, she mentioned she was waiting for an application.

"What kind of application?" I asked, taking the bait.

"Oh," she said, pausing to take a deep breath. "I asked one of the nuns if there were any openings for new students at their private high school in Salem, Massachusetts."

She tried to feign nonchalance, as if she were just suggesting I go to a friend's house for an afternoon.

"What?" I asked.

I had already started making plans with my friends for my upcoming freshman year at Stephens High School, the local public school.

"Why would you send me to a nunnery?"

This school, St. Chretienne Academy, had a reputation for being very strict. It was a boarding school for young women considering a life in the nunnery and a feeder program for the real thing. In some ways, it was a fishing expedition, looking to see how many potential candidates they could catch.

Short on answers, my mother reminded me that in the second grade, I had a doll dressed as a nun.

"So?" I continued in disbelief. "It was a gift."

This gift had come from Sister Thérèse, my mother's sibling who had become a nun at the age of nineteen. The doll she sent me for Christmas was meant to be a carbon copy of herself, a sweet gesture—but accepting the gift didn't obligate me to a life in the nunnery. I had no interest in following in my aunt's foot-steps, but the wheels were already in motion. It hardly mattered whether I liked it or not.

"I think somewhere in your head, you have always wanted to be a nun," my mother said.

The truth was *she* wanted me to be a nun and was on her way to making it so.

"Mom, that's crazy!"

"Well, I want you to give it some thought," she said, her tone making it clear that the conversation was over. Her mind was made up, and within a week my application was sent and her plan was put into action.

In no time, I received a letter of acceptance accompanied by two lists of items—things I could have and a much longer list of things I could not. The "acceptable" list was called my "trousseau." I didn't like the sound of that. Black stockings, black shoes, and black uniforms were not just allowed but required. I was not allowed to bring jewelry, makeup, hair accessories, or street clothing. Personal

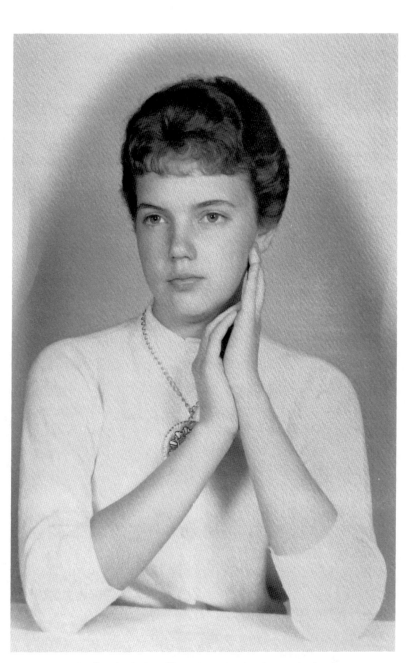

A formal portrait of me in the late fifties about the time I started school at
St. Chretienne Academy.

photos, books, and diaries were not allowed. I was forbidden to have outside contact with anyone except my immediate family, and only by letter, once a month—and those letters would be read by one of the nuns before I was allowed to see them.

I would have to leave everything and everyone from my present life and focus solely on becoming a nun. I even had to give up my name, trading it in for an identifying number: I would be known henceforth as number 24. The few things I was allowed to possess would all be labeled in cross-stitch and black marker with that number.

On a warm day at the end of August, my mother drove south on the turnpike and deposited me at the nunnery in Salem, the town of pilgrims, witches, and, apparently, nuns.

I was terrified, but I knew there was no turning back. My family had been humiliated by divorce, and I was being sent to a convent to become something I didn't want to be.

"I know you are going to like convent life," my mother told me. She had spent her high school years in a convent too, but it wasn't as strict as this one was. Her plan for my life was playing out, and there was nothing I could do about it. I was being left behind in a convent, alone. Although she attempted to paint a positive picture, the truth was she had no idea what was about to happen to me.

The good sisters were waiting when we arrived and greeted me with open arms and rapacious smiles. I was a new recruit and they recognized my value.

"Give it your best shot, honey," my mother said cheerily as she slammed the door to our old yellow Studebaker. This probably wasn't easy for her, either. I knew how tired and overwhelmed she felt. I had heard her crying at night.

She kissed me on the cheek and left, not wanting to give me any opportunity to get back into the car.

As I watched her drive down the long cedar-lined driveway and disappear, I felt abandoned. There I was, with my black clothes and my overwhelming feelings of impending doom. It would have been easy to cry, but I resolved not to. I wouldn't let anyone know how bad I felt. I had been left alone in a strange city without family or friends, and I was expected to figure things out on my own and, eventually, become a nun.

As number 24, I would try.

I was thirteen.

My father had left, and now, my mother had too.

Four

Copper Crucifix

Everyone in my new world dressed in black. I trailed a diminutive nun along endless hallways, through dim rooms decorated with portraits of popes, past and present. Christ, of course, was everywhere—hanging on walls, resting on pedestals, appearing in paintings, statues, and carvings.

The bedroom I was assigned was painted powder blue and furnished with four iron-frame twin beds, painted the same color as the room, and a single chair placed beside each bed along with a couple of religious prints. Each bed had a thin blanket folded with cold precision at the foot. No pretense of comfort. No effort to feel welcoming.

The nun who'd led me to my room said, "We have a strict code of silence here. You may only speak freely from three to four in the afternoon, during snack time. If you need to speak before or after that, you must first ask for permission."

This stranger now controlled every aspect of my life and was telling me that conversation would have to be scheduled. Number 24 could only speak out loud and hear her own voice from three to four in the afternoon.

"Dinner is at seven p.m.," she continued, "and we take turns reading the Gospel during dinner. Remember: God is always watching, and he will know if you break the code of silence."

With that, she left the room. It was the start of my indoctrination and the belief that God knew every move I made.

Two of the girls I shared the room with have faded beyond memory, but the third has a forever place in the deep recesses of my mind. She was an older girl I knew from home named Gabriella, and in the time since I'd last seen her, she'd become a bona fide religious zealot.

"I'm surprised to see you in the convent, Terry," she whispered.

"I'm surprised to see you here as well," I answered, violating the code of silence five minutes after I'd learned it existed.

My mind flashed back to the summertime adventures Gabriella and I had shared. We'd created our own summer theater program, neighborhood Broadway at its finest, with a performance stage and musical events. We choreographed routines, learned lyrics to all the latest songs, and acted out music and dialogue to our hearts' content.

Gabriella was a connection to home, and for that, I was grateful. I would soon realize the Gabriella I'd known was all but gone, replaced by a girl who wanted not only to become a nun but to become a martyr.

"I've been called here to suffer for Christ," she said in lofty tones, placing special emphasis on the word "suffer" and pointing her nose heavenward, a devout snob. I knew what a martyr was, and the fact Gabriella desired so strongly to die for Jesus confused and frightened me. Did she have a plan?

Would I have to watch her martyr herself?

My first night in the convent, I learned that Gabriella had a copper crucifix hidden under her bedcovers. She had taken the crucifix from her grandmother's coffin after the funeral and slept with it every night, the way a different child might sleep with a teddy bear. Gabriella, it turned out, had more than one secret. In addition to the contraband crucifix, she also cut herself at night while the rest of us slept, creating wounds she hoped to pass off as stigmata, bodily wounds or scars in locations corresponding to the crucification wounds of Christ. She imagined being recognized as a living miracle, a saint with bleeding symbols of the cross on her arms. She kept her wounds hidden under the long black sleeves of her uniform as she worked to create the effect. The rest of us stayed out of Gabriella's way, lest she bring the wrath of that crucifix down upon us or else infect us somehow with her crazed brand of religious devotion.

At night, I waited until Gabriella had fallen asleep before I dared to sleep myself. The comfort of knowing someone from home was short-lived. When Gabriella left the convent a year later, taking the copper crucifix with her, I was relieved. As it turned out, crucifix or no, she would become neither a nun nor a martyr, although she would live a somewhat solitary life.

Daily, as we walked the long corridors of the nunnery in perfectly straight lines, we recited endless loops of prayer in both Latin and French. The small chapel where we attended early-morning Mass was quiet and smelled of burning wax. On some days, Mass was followed by a visit to the confessional.

Located at the back of the chapel, the confessional was a brown wooden box with a center door. It looked ominous, like a portal to some forbidding place. Faded red velvet curtains drooped on the outside, and inside, a small sliding wooden screen door was all that separated the sinner from the priest. There was a single lightbulb in the center of the confessional so the priest could read while waiting for more sins to absolve. We knelt patiently in the last pew waiting for him to whisper, "Enter."

At thirteen, I understood sin was an act that broke any of the Ten Commandments. Did that mean degrees of brokenness or was it just black-and-white? I didn't know. If I wasn't breaking any Commandments, what were my sins? Nothing I did seemed to qualify for my definition of sin, and I didn't feel like a sinner, so I had to pretend that I was.

The nuns were more than happy to provide us with reasons why we needed absolution.

"It's a sacrament, dear," Sister Augustine said. "It will shower you with extra spiritual grace. Look into your soul, and you will find many things for which you need to be forgiven."

I was in no position to argue with her, but it was never easy for me to go to the confessional. To sit in the semi-darkness and bare my soul to a complete stranger was a challenge. The priest would turn his head and look intimately through you, anticipating every word.

"Bless me, Father, for I have sinned" was the introductory phrase we were taught to use. Other "sinners" waited outside the box for their opportunity to confess, so we whispered in a futile attempt at privacy.

As I sat there in contemplation, there was definite pressure and expectation. What had I done in the last few days that would be Commandment breakers when every minute of my life was monitored by the nuns? I decided if I couldn't identify any, I would have to make them up.

"Father, I accuse myself of eating two sandwiches." That would cover the sin of gluttony, I surmised. I became inventive, making up sins so I would get the benefit of the grace the nuns had promised and not be embarrassed if I didn't have any. Collecting Grace was like collecting points in a game. The more Grace points you had, the better your chances were to reach the ultimate goal of getting to heaven. They were a ticket to salvation.

At the end of the recitation, the priest would issue his punishment: "Say three Hail Marys and one Our Father."

I would then be free to walk out of the confessional, assured that whatever sins I had committed were wiped clean. For a few minutes, at least, I was a walking example of purity.

Every minute in the convent was part of a strict routine. Up at six in the morning, wash, dress, pray, and eat. Dressed identically in black, we sat in silence at meals while someone read the catechism. Classes, chores, confession. Each moment accounted for, every decision made for us, every day the same. The goal was to prepare us for a life of poverty, chastity, and obedience. The very idea of being an individual, of having an identity, was to be ground out of us. Everything was done in the service of the collective. Even though there were girls attending the school who lived off campus and were not in training to be a nun, we could not interact with them in classes (some had as many as thirty girls) or on the grounds during the day.

For some of the girls, this seemed to work.

As time passed, however, I knew it wasn't working for me. I had no choice about being there, but each day brought me closer to a time when I would.

Five

When Enough is Enough

Sister Augustine handed me a simple white cotton gown with instructions. "Wear this when you take your bath," she said. "It is not permitted to look at your own naked body in the bathtub."

On Saturday mornings, the convent was quiet. The nuns were busy catching up with their own personal weekly chores, and they left us alone, warning that God was more than capable of taking over the job of monitoring us for a few hours. *He* would be their eyes and ears.

I didn't believe everything the nuns told me, but I did believe that God knew everything and he would know immediately if I let my mind stray into sinful thoughts. That was where the cotton bathing gown came in. If I couldn't see my developing body, the logic went, then I couldn't have impure thoughts about it.

Sister Augustine brought a whole stack of neatly folded white cotton gowns, and, in addition to the bath, I was to use them to cover my body as I dressed for the day. She demonstrated how to do this as she talked.

"Take your arms out of the sleeves and put your day clothes on like this," she said, showing me how to dress and undress under the gown without seeing any of my own body. It took some time to do this as effortlessly as Sister Augustine, but I managed it. For the next two years, I was afraid to look at my own breasts, lest I should be committing a sin in the eyes of God.

As strictly as the convent was run, there were still opportunities to have a little taste of freedom. My friend Evie and I discovered an attic quite by accident as we finished our chores one Saturday morning. On my own, I would have just finished my work and gone to lunch, but Evie was more adventurous than me—and more desperate for the slightest semblance of self-determination. She hated every minute she spent in the convent.

"Let's go take a look," she said.

I thought immediately of Sister Augustine, our direct supervisor and a no-nonsense kind of guardian. We feared her. She barely had to speak. Standing in place, with her broad hips and big feet spread wide, her presence was enough to convince us to do as we were told. Usually. On the other hand, Sister Augustine was nowhere in sight, having left us to our work as she did every Saturday.

"Evie, if we get caught we could be in serious trouble," I said.

"What's the worst that could happen?"

"We could get kicked out," I said.

She grabbed my arm and pushed me up the stairs.

On tiptoe, we moved across the attic, making a pathway in the dust; clearly no one had been up there in a very long time. The convent was built on top of a hill, isolating us from the world that existed beyond its walls, but a small window at the peak of the roof gave us a panoramic view of the city. Somehow, that view was enough to inspire hope that our time there would, sooner or later, come to an end and that the world would be waiting for us when it did. As teenage girls, we wanted to talk about life and boys and the changes we were going through, and in the attic, for a short time, we could do just that. Soon, visiting the attic became a regular Saturday morning activity.

On most weekends, the landscaper brought his teenaged son to help with the maintenance of the convent gardens. He often worked shirtless, and we cleaned the dirt away from the window-pane to watch him flex his muscles as he cleaned the flower beds and walkways around the convent.

One Saturday morning, he looked up and discovered us staring at him. Rather than seeming alarmed or pointing us out to his father, he merely tipped his hat in our direction. He was as curious about us as we were about him. Although we never did meet or have a conversation, we felt a connection to him. In the privation of the convent, just a silent acknowledgment from a boy felt like an illicit affair.

If I hadn't known it before, those Saturday mornings in the attic made me realize that life in a nunnery was not for me. I had never heard the "calling" that others spoke of—I'd just been forced to go there by my mother. And contrary to what she'd told me the day she dropped me off, I never came to like life at the convent.

The nuns weren't happy when I announced in April that I wouldn't return the following September. They had invested two years in me, and they weren't willing to let me go without a fight. For the next few months, Sister Augustine visited my bedroom every night as the clock in the hallway struck nine. It was the witches' hour, and she, dressed entirely in black, would swish in and out of my dark bedroom under the pretense of a bed check, whispering in my ear, "God led you here for a special reason, and to act against God's will and leave would be a serious mistake."

Her voice had a gravelly sound, and she called me by my French name, MarieThérèse, which elevated her words to a more serious level. She made it sound as though God himself had sent her to deliver this message.

I was afraid to fall asleep, thinking that Sister Augustine would lock me in a dark room somewhere in the convent and leave me there. I started pretending to be asleep when she made her nightly bed check.

After several months of this, I made my decision and placed an emergency call to my mother. "I'm not staying here, Mom," I said. "I don't have a vocation, and I don't want to be a nun. I want a life. This was your idea, and I gave it two full years. I'm coming home in June and I'm not coming back."

I used the same tone of authority in my voice that the nuns used on us.

"Okay," my mother said. "Finish the year, and that will be enough."

I almost couldn't believe it. Two years of my life, and that's all she had to say?

I was happy, of course, but also wondered why, if it had been so important that I go to the convent in the first place, it was so easy for her to agree that my time there had come to an end.

By the time June arrived and my sophomore year was finished, I had my suitcase under my bed, packed and ready to go. After two full years in the convent, Mother returned to collect me, and this time, when the old yellow Studebaker drove down the cedar-lined driveway, I was in it, heading home.

Six

The River

One day after I returned to Rumford, I got it in my head to see my hometown from the perspective of the Androscoggin River, something I'd never done. I don't know where I got the idea to do this, but I talked my younger brother, Rick, into borrowing a canoe and paddling down the river with me.

"Come on," I said. "Let's borrow a canoe so we can go out on the river."

It was a beautiful Saturday, and I was determined.

"I don't think Mom would let us go," my brother said. He was cautious and didn't want to upset anyone.

"Well, let's not tell her then," I said.

He finally gave in, and we found ourselves in a red canoe, sitting in the middle of the river, with no real idea what we were doing.

Being out on the Androscoggin gave me a broader—and darker—view of my town and the papermaking industry. It was an awakening that caught me off guard.

I didn't know our beautiful river was being used as a sewer by every community and mill along its 160-mile length. I saw old pipes discharging smelly brown wastewater. It was puzzling to see rich green foliage arching along the riverway and yet have the offensive stink of rotten-egg gas assaulting our noses. As we paddled along, toilet paper hung on the oars, and floating tin cans and tires bumped the canoe's hull. The river was, in effect, a landfill and toxic waste dump all in one.

One of my oars got tangled in an old trench coat. I wondered if a body was floating below the murky, foam-flecked surface. Like Lewis and Clark, we were traveling into a world unfamiliar to us, except the water we were crossing was poisoned and dirty. The industrial end product looked like foam and collected in all the small inlets along the way as it crept its way downriver, dragged along by the current from one town to the next. One Maine farmer described this toxic foam as "too thick to paddle, too thin to plow."

It was the sixties, still years away from when Sen. Edmund Muskie would spearhead the groundbreaking Clean Water Act, which passed in 1972. Like me, Muskie grew up in Rumford and he already knew about the environmental damage my brother and I were discovering that Saturday morning.

My brother and I vowed to return to the river with a barge to collect the debris left behind, but we never did. Still, I would never forget this perspective or my day on the river.

Seven

Stephens High School

After two years of (relative) silence behind convent walls, the noise and bustle of Rumford's Stephens High School was a shock to my system. Most other students thought I was just shy, and I was to an extent, but I was also awash in sensory overload. For two years, I was conditioned to be silent, to speak only at certain times—to have neither a personal voice nor an opinion. I was trained to be obedient and quiet, and although I secretly chafed against these restrictions, I also internalized them. I simply was not prepared for life as a teenager in a public high school.

By that time I was a junior and I quickly discovered my old friends had found new friends. Standing alone was something I had become familiar with, and although I made new friends, I became close to only a few. Mostly, I just listened and played catch-up.

It was the sixties, so in our school, the topic of the Vietnam War raged, often in heated discussions I never could have imagined at the convent.

"I'm going to enlist," Jimmy Boudreaux whispered to me one day in English class.

"Why would you do that, Jimmy?" I asked. "Don't do it! You're too young."

"I'll be eighteen in March, and I'm going to sign up right after graduation," Jimmy said defiantly, looking at me as though I were suddenly his enemy.

Jimmy made good on his promise and enlisted, leaving for basic training right after graduation. He expected to be sent to Vietnam.

"Good luck, Jimmy," we said in class, hugging him for the last time. He was a small kid, and I could feel his ribs in that hug. Caught up in the patriotic flurry about the war, he was willing to serve in a way that wasn't really about protecting his own country. Then he was gone, and none of us would see him alive again.

He died slowly, first losing both legs to a land mine and then losing his life to infection. His remains were put on display in a casket lined in white satin. Handsome in life, he was the same in death, despite his missing body parts, a tribute to another local undertaker.

Much later in my life, I visited the Vietnam Veterans Memorial in Washington, DC and found Jimmy's name written among the nearly sixty thousand others. I trembled and wept as I ran my fingers over his name etched deep in the granite surface. I wished Jimmy had made a different choice. But he didn't. He bought a big lie and died for it.

I later came to understand that many others in our town bought a different big lie and were dying for that as well. When I think about Jimmy's sacrifice, and compare it to the many in Rumford who died from the consequences of exposure to toxic chemicals, it doesn't seem all that different to me. Seeing the cancer cases that resulted from this exposure etched in granite would be an equally impressive visual reminder.

The paper industry told us all that whatever was coming out of those towering smokestacks was harmless. It wasn't.

During this time, when I was trying to decide the direction my life would take, I became aware of the work of Dr. Thomas Dooley. Dooley worked tirelessly to treat and save thousands of refugees in Southeast Asia. *Time, Life, Look,* and *Newsweek* magazines presented full layouts of a tall, lanky, handsome young physician dripping with poetic words and photos in feature articles entitled "The Splendid American," "Do it Yourself Samaritan," and "The Schweitzer of Asia." He was a familiar and favorite guest on radio and television talk shows, including popular programs hosted by Arthur Godfrey, where Dooley would tell stories about his life in the jungle and the work at his medical clinics. Known as "the jungle doctor," his books and lectures were widely publicized, and his book *The Edge of Tomorrow* became my favorite. I read it multiple times and felt I somehow had a personal connection to his story.

I sent my hard-earned babysitting money to his foundation, MEDICO. Although he was later criticized and accused of exaggerating his jungle stories, I knew nothing of this at the time. When he died of malignant melanoma on my birthday, it felt as though I had lost a family member. I cried thinking how short his life had been and how his mission had come to such an abrupt end.

I'd wanted to be a nurse for as long as I could remember, going all the way back to the days when it was my job to press and starch my mother's nursing uniforms. Reading about Dooley and his life of service solidified my ambition. The idea of personal service was one useful thing I learned in the convent, and I believed Thomas Dooley had lived that life.

I wanted to do the same.

I graduated in the spring of 1963, helping to write lyrics to our graduation song, sung to the popular 1953 tune *Moulin Rouge*. At the graduation ceremony I played Beethoven's *Sonata Pathétique* on the piano between speeches and tears. My grandfather, who was also my piano teacher, sat in the audience. I studied with him from the age of seven, and although everyone called him the Professor, to me he was *pépère* (the French word for grandfather). He was proud of my performance that day. Years of piano studies with him made me shine. And then it was over. High school was behind me and the future, bright but uncertain, lay ahead.

Eight

Nursing 101

Even though I left the convent, the Catholic Church remained, in many regards, the central entity in my world. My aunts, cousins, and friends served the Church as nuns, teachers, nurses, musicians, altar boys, and prayerful followers of a religion I no longer believed in. Although I had been a good student of religion, professing beliefs every Sunday in church, the two years I spent in the convent changed my view on religion forever.

Perhaps it was curious, then, that I applied to a Catholic nursing school, but I did. I filled out an application, got a few personal letters of recommendation, and secured a personal interview at the Mercy Hospital School of Nursing in Portland. It was my first choice, and I was accepted.

While becoming a nurse was a dream, I guess an even bigger dream was to study music at Boston College. I envisioned myself following in my grandfather's footsteps as a Church musician, studying in the great European cathedrals. But I had no money and I didn't know how to do it.

And I also wanted to be a nurse. When Rumford Community Hospital announced the criteria for its annual scholarship, I applied and qualified. A full tuition scholarship only required one thing—that you return after graduation and work for one year. The scholarship gave me a pathway to follow and made furthering my education possible. For that, I was grateful.

When my letter of acceptance arrived, I was confident that my life was finally moving in a direction I wanted. In the sixties, nursing was a profession dominated by women, with Florence Nightingale as the archetype. Men mostly became physicians, and although some chose nursing as a career, few crossed those barriers at the time. The Mercy nursing school had a curriculum divided into three-month rotations. All rotations were local except for psychiatry, which took place in Baltimore.

The idea of traveling to Baltimore seemed adventurous, and, as a naive nineteen-year-old, I found being in the middle of a large and vibrant city eye-popping. Judy was my roommate. We met as freshmen. On our first day of class, discussing the principles of Nursing 101, we quickly became friends and were assigned the Baltimore rotation at the same time. On the nine-hour bus ride, Judy and I shared our dreams about our careers, future travel plans, and our lives as a whole. We watched the landscape of the Eastern Seaboard roll up and disappear behind us, and before we knew it, we were in Baltimore, ready to begin our psych rotation.

Everything I owned fit into one small suitcase, so unpacking was simple. Uniforms were issued by the hospital. The dorms were bare, offering a place to sleep at the end of the day and little more. The rooms were on a long corridor that had a single forty-watt bulb giving off just enough light to see the length of the dark, gloomy hallway. Located at the far end from my room was a single pay phone that was used by all thirty girls living on the floor.

The weather was hot in Baltimore even though it was still early spring—wildly different from the cold, wet, spring weather of my New England town. No question, escaping a long, cold, and snowy winter was something we looked forward to, and Baltimore didn't disappoint.

One night, not long after we'd arrived, Judy announced there was a dance in the ballroom that evening. She was excited. I wasn't.

Every dorm had a housemother who made sure everyone was in their rooms by curfew, locked up the dorm at night, and provided occasional entertainment for restless young nursing students far from home. On this Saturday night, our housemother had arranged to have a busload of young men trucked in for a dance. They came from army bases, local colleges, and medical schools.

The flyer read like an advertisement: "Dance tonight. Nursing students visiting Baltimore looking for dance partners." I didn't like it—it sounded as if we were being offered up like cattle—but Judy persisted. She didn't want to go alone and was relentless in her pleading. Eventually I gave in. I showered, dressed quickly, and, with my hair still damp, I was ready.

Joined by two other girls from our newly arrived group, we were about to enter a new chapter of our lives.

I had never really spent time in a city, and the buildings in Baltimore were stunning. It was an old city, and the ballroom reflected this history. The stairway was embellished with ornate carvings of oak and mahogany, and I pretended I was Scarlett O'Hara as I walked down this dramatic staircase to make my entrance into the grand ballroom. Coming from a blue-collar mill town, I had never seen anything like the ballroom, or the dance it held, and certainly had never made an entrance in this way. It felt like a big moment.

A young man, Wayne, approached me just as I reached the ballroom floor.

"May I have the next dance?" he asked, waking me from my *Gone with the Wind* fantasy. Later, Wayne told me he fell in love with me at that very moment and knew he would eventually ask for my hand in marriage.

I was less certain.

Nonetheless, I danced every dance with him, and when he asked for my telephone number, I gave it to him.

Nine

The Rule of the Keys

Orientation started early the morning after the dance with a tour of the hospital and a set of keys. We toured everything behind locked doors, then lectures about maintaining our safety took up the rest of the day. Nursing care in a psychiatric hospital in the sixties was different from that in a regular medical-surgical type of hospital. This place was managed by the same order of nuns that managed the hospital in Maine. Some of the nursing staff were nuns; others were not. For three long days, we sat and listened.

They taught us to recognize signs and symptoms of escalating anxiety in psychiatric patients. Some patients were in isolation because they presented a danger to themselves or others. Living in an alternate reality where straitjackets were common, they were locked in rooms with padded walls. Others who were considered more trustworthy, at least in theory, were free to walk about as long as they stayed in the lockdown unit. With no concept of reality, they didn't know who or where they were.

I was terrified by all of it. No experience prepared me for what I saw on that psychiatric ward, but it was part of my training to get used to it and work effectively.

"Don't take any of their behavior personally," said Sister Mary Jo, the nun assigned to new students. "You can't be friends with anyone here. These are your patients and your responsibility while you are on duty and nothing more."

Some patients were my age, which made me even more anxious.

The "Rule of Keys" was the first thing Sister Mary Jo taught us during orientation.

"These keys can be used as both a weapon and a source of power," she said. "Patients respect the nurses with keys. This key is the master key. It will lock and unlock every door coming in and going out. This funny-shaped one is only for the nurses' station, and this little one unlocks the drug cupboard. All of them are important. You will need to have them in your possession at all times and be ready to use them."

I was beginning to understand the danger in this rotation. I never liked violence, so the idea of a physical encounter made me uncomfortable. As in other nursing rotations, the instructors encouraged us to consider psychiatric nursing as a career path, but I wasn't interested. This was just something I had to get through, a means to an end, although I would end up using the skills acquired in psychiatric nursing throughout my career.

Every unit was staffed by at least one orderly. Mostly strong men, they acted as a buffer between a combative patient and a nurse. They also helped lift and move patients who had been stationary for too long and were unable to do much for themselves.

My first assigned patient, Miss Janes, was a woman who had been abused in every imaginable way. Raped at twelve and left for dead, she found escape in a fantasy world that she could control. She hissed at me like a feral cat when I met her, lunging toward me in an aggressive stance. I stepped back as the orderly cautioned, "Careful—this one can be dangerous."

If I didn't know before, Miss Janes made it clear that I was in over my head. I would have to find, or develop, some serious confidence if I wanted to graduate.

I liked the romance of being a nurse and the inspiration of Thomas Dooley, but I also choose nursing as a career because I was offered a full scholarship. I had nothing to fall back on, and the scholarship disappeared if I couldn't hack the psych rotation. Scared and insecure as I was, I needed to make it work.

But the situation at hand was escalating. Miss Janes was uncomfortable with change, and seeing new faces was threatening to her. The orderly restrained her and brought her back to the quiet safety of her room. She was psychotic, and after a lifetime of abuse, she saw danger everywhere. She lashed out, preferring to hurt instead of being hurt. Who could blame her? I'd read her chart and it wasn't pretty.

The nurse in charge heard the commotion and quickly came to see what was happening. But she was careless in her haste, and Miss Janes suddenly grabbed her by the throat and threatened to kill her.

The orderly managed to pull Miss Janes away from the nursing supervisor and place her back into restraints. It was an ugly physical battle, and I wasn't sure who was winning. There was nothing for me to do. I was scared. I stood there, feeling helpless.

"Get a sedative," the nurse in charge shouted at me. She used a firm voice, attempting to control her own fear. She had been through this before.

As she stood up, trying to regain her composure, her starched white nursing cap tilted to the side of her head, giving her a disheveled look. For a split second, I saw the tilted cap as a bit of comedy, but there was nothing funny about any of this.

Glad to have a job to do, I rushed to the nurses' station and the medicine cabinet. I found the master key that locked and unlocked every door along the way, and despite my shaking hands and wobbly knees, I managed to extract the exact amount of sedative from the multi-dose vial needed to quiet Miss Janes.

When I returned, both the orderly and the nursing supervisor held Miss Janes while I thrust the needle into her upper thigh. I don't think she even felt it, but in no time, she was ready for a nap. With the incident defused, we all returned to the regular plan for the day.

This might have been the first time I'd felt truly connected to my profession—like it was a job I could do and do well. There had been a problem and I had done my part to solve it. I felt empowered, newly competent.

This wouldn't last long.

At the nurses' station, I was told that all current treatments—except one—had been tried on Miss Janes, but none had been successful. The next option was electroshock therapy, a last resort that, owing to its brutality, was saved for only the most hopeless patients. Miss Janes qualified and would receive her first treatment the following day.

To prepare myself, I read all I could find in my textbooks about electroshock. When I finished reading, I imagined I was ready. I wasn't. I've never been able to escape the memory of what happened the next morning.

Miss Janes arrived in the treatment room by stretcher, bound in a straitjacket. She was lifted to a flat table covered with a starched white sheet, and the straitjacket was removed. Her arms and legs were secured to the table by thick, worn, brown leather straps. A sweaty smell came from tightening the straps. The smell of old leather still brings me back to this moment.

Miss Janes fought the restraints with every ounce of her ninety-five pounds. It took two orderlies to hold her in place. A padded tongue depressor was set horizontally in her mouth to keep her from biting or swallowing her tongue. Although mildly sedated, her eyes still registered fear. She was trapped, and she knew it. I was afraid, too, and in some odd way, I felt on display. As a student nurse, my performance would be recorded, and it would be part of my evaluation at the end of the three-month rotation.

Sister Mary Jo's words played over and over again in my head. "Don't show any emotion," she warned. "Above all else, you must remain professional. No noise and no facial expressions. Remain in place, be helpful if you are asked, but be a part of the setting and nothing more."

I tried to pretend none of this bothered me, but it wasn't true. Everyone but me had seen this procedure before, I was a novice and the only student in the room. I would do what I had done before—store the memory of these events in a dark corner of my mind, write about it in my journal, and deal with it at a later time.

"All clear," the technician announced in a calm, firm voice.

Everyone stepped back from the treatment table as he adjusted the knobs on the machine to the prescribed voltage and pushed the on button. We watched as electricity shot through Miss Janes, her small body seizing up instantly. She arched into a U shape. Her eyes were open and registered both pain and fear. Her jaw clenched with enough force to snap the tongue depressor in two. Thick white foam dripped from the corners of her mouth, and although nothing was burning, a smell of intense heat filled the room.

When the electric current stopped, she lay limp and unconscious but breathing in a regular rhythm. Only the ticking of the clock gave me a sense of place, while the near silence kept us locked in time. All of this took only a few minutes, but it felt like an eternity.

We brought Miss Janes, asleep and unrestrained, back to her room on the same stretcher she'd arrived on. Everyone but me moved with a hurried callousness, as there was another patient already queued up for the same treatment.

I was relieved when my ten-hour shift ended and I could return to my dorm room.

In my room Judy was waiting for me and handed me a small piece of white paper with a phone number. It was Wayne's.

"Looks like he was smitten," she chirped. "So, what do you think about dorm dances now?"

I was too emotionally spent to have this conversation with Judy, but I thought it would be rude not to return Wayne's call. I walked to the end of the long dark hallway to the single pay phone and dialed the number Judy had scribbled on paper.

He answered on the first ring.

"I remembered that Saturday is your day off and you wanted to tour the Capitol," Wayne said. "We'll leave early. Wear sneakers."

Ten

Tricky Dick

Saturday came and went as quickly as most things do that are
anticipated. I didn't wear sneakers, thinking they would look
awkward with my new sundress, opting for sandals instead. Wayne
picked me up in his vintage sports car for a day filled with animated conversation. As we toured the nation's capital city sitting
low in green leather bucket seats, we spoke of our life's dreams.

It was our first date and our first impressions of each other
outside of the ballroom where we'd met. I genuinely liked him.
He was carefree and fun. The eldest of nine children, he was both
confident and kind. Wayne, who had grown up in Maryland,
had majored in political science in college, so it was no surprise
to learn that he was keenly interested in the issues of the day.
His blue eyes sparkled when he smiled, and his handshake was
genuine. He was fully present with me, giving equal time to both
listening and talking. I had been talked at a lot in my lifetime, so
having someone listen to what I had to say was a new experience.

Wayne grew up in politics, coming through the ranks of a
group called the Young Republicans. As a political feeder group,
they recruited only the best and the brightest from high schools

51

and colleges, at least according to the description outlined in their brochure. This was how he became interested in government. He worked for a large insurance company, with strategic planning as his strong suit and politics as his passion.

Our views couldn't have been more different. While we did share mutual interests, in politics, we were opposites. I was particularly interested in environmental issues and, while visiting Washington, decided that I would try to meet Ed Muskie, a Democrat who had been governor of Maine from 1955 to 1959 and had been a US Senator since 1959.

Muskie, born in Rumford in 1914, was a first-generation American—his father immigrated to Rumford from Poland, back when Rumford was a roaring and exciting place to be. As a boy, Ed Muskie would sit on his porch, deep in conversation with his father, discussing issues and ideas brought from the "Old Country." He was eager to learn, and these conversations educated him about things beyond the cradle of the mountain valley. Serving as a US Senator until 1980, Muskie became one of the most powerful men in government.

Muskie tried to make industry listen—to put the brakes on pollution and do the right thing for everyone, including the people of our shared hometown who worked at the paper mill. His signature pieces of legislation would come a few years later: The Clean Air Act of 1970 and The Clean Water Act of 1972. The Clean Water Act was the primary federal law regarding pollution in the nation's waters, including the Androscoggin.

I did manage to shake his hand as he made his way through the halls of Congress on that trip. Although I'm sure he forgot that handshake as soon as it happened, I remember it to this day. On this one particular day in my lifetime, I had the opportunity to view the largeness of the world and to meet a man who had found a way to make a difference. I felt older and wiser and more connected to a life I had only dreamed of.

Like Muskie, I had always been interested in environmental issues. I loved my hometown but hated the familiar smell of caustic chemicals that invaded everything. I couldn't name them yet, but I knew the way they made me feel. There was a sourness to the air; on bad days my eyes burned and taking a deep breath made my lungs ache. It was hard to understand how the land could be so lush and green and the air so toxic at the same time.

In Rumford, my life was defined by circles. Located dead center at the bottom of a bowl, my town was isolated within a ring of tall granite mountains. In the middle of my world stood a 412-foot-tall emission tower that dominated the visual center of the town. Trapped within the concentric circles of this industry, we were held hostage in a paternalistic, corporate universe.

The word "tower" conjures up an image of elevation. This tower, unlike the Tower of London, was actually a chimney that burned a mixture of chipped tires, paper mill sludge, and coal and wood waste. It was built high enough for the blowers to send emissions from the burning chimney out of our valley into the neighboring towns. It was a scheme that didn't always work, creating a false sense of security within the town. Yes, there was burning, they said, but the emissions went somewhere else; and besides, they were harmless anyway. Many would believe this lie, not because it seemed true, but because they wanted it to be.

During his time as a political activist, Upton Sinclair wrote, "It is difficult to get a man to understand something when his salary depends on his not understanding it." From his reasearch for *The Jungle*, a novel exposing labor and sanitary conditions in the meatpacking industry, Sinclair knew what the worker was up against and grasped that the allure of the devil's bargain—your health for steady work and good pay—was powerful.

The chimney idea wasn't a perfect system. With an air inversion, the black soot that was blown up into the sky would fall back onto our neighborhoods as particulate matter. The air had no lift, and the inversion created dead air, allowing the ash to fall, landing like black pepper over the entire town. Everything was dirty all the time. We made plans according to which way the wind was blowing. If the chemical fog hung low in a downdraft, we stayed indoors and the windows remained shut. Most saw this as the cost of doing business—the smell of money. A kind of willful intellectual disability took over whenever a paycheck was involved.

Wayne was certainly interested in my stories of small-town pollution, but he didn't understand it and I think had a hard time believing what I told him. Why wouldn't he be skeptical? He hadn't grown up breathing polluted air and swimming in toxic waters.

"I have a question for you," he said. "There is a major political event happening Saturday evening and I would like you to be my date."

He was shy about asking and I liked that. He took nothing for granted. There was a sweetness about him I found endearing.

"Sure," I answered, trying not to sound as eager as I felt.

It was the mid-sixties and Wayne, as president of the Young Republicans, was hosting a reception for Richard Nixon. Nixon, who served as vice president under Dwight Eisenhower in the fifties and lost a close presidential race to John F. Kennedy in 1960, would run for president again in 1968. Spiro Agnew, who would become governor of Maryland in 1967 and then be chosen as Nixon's running mate in 1968, was also a headliner at the event. Their two leading politicians, one a local Baltimore man and the other a former vice president, brought a lot of excitement to the gala.

My growing curiosity about the political issues of the day kept us in conversation all the way back to the dorm. Wayne opened the door, took my hand and kissed it, and said, "See you at seven on Saturday night." My heart flip-flopped as I left him, already thinking about Saturday night.

I fussed all week about what to wear. It wasn't a black-tie event, but I wanted to look elegant. With just enough basic clothing for a few months' rotation, my wardrobe wasn't up to the task. My dorm friends came to the rescue, gathering some of their own favorite pieces of clothing to share with me. It wouldn't take long to transform me from a hardworking student nurse to a sophisticated young woman on her way to a historic political evening.

I chose an understated black A-line dress and a single strand of pearls.

"Be careful with the pearls," Alice said. "They belonged to my grandmother!"

Judy styled my hair in a French twist. A final look in the bedroom mirror pleased me.

Wayne picked me up promptly at seven and I watched my friends waving from the second-story windows.

"Wow! You look terrific," he said with a smile that took up his entire face.

"Thanks," I remember saying, while thinking about what it took for my dorm friends to accomplish my Cinderella transformation.

We arrived at the event rather early. While Wayne was greeting the press and early guests, I was free to roam about the venue. I found my name card placed in a seating arrangement I didn't like and changed it. I'd never liked the limelight. I was used to sitting in the background at events. I wanted to sit in a place where I could observe everything and not be seen, so I chose a seat with my back to the wall. It gave me a perfect view of the podium and the entire room. Wayne was appropriately attentive, dividing his time between his responsibilities and me.

Except for my visit with Muskie the previous week, the closest I had ever come to meeting a real politician was at the Fourth of July picnic in my town. Both Democrat and Republican candidates would show up to eat hot dogs, fried dough, and cotton candy together while expounding on their views of how to run the government.

When Nixon arrived early, Wayne brought him over to meet me. After a few pleasantries, Nixon pulled out a chair and sat down. "Wayne tells me that you're a state of Maine Republican," he said.

I wasn't a Republican, but it didn't seem prudent to correct him. Nixon delivered an impressive soliloquy, rambling on as politicians do. He was used to having people listen to him. I started to feel some discomfort at his level of attention as he shifted to asking personal questions. He was alone that evening, and I was in the middle of my psychiatric rotation, alert to the idiosyncrasies of individual personality behaviors. Dick Nixon didn't escape that evaluation. There was an oddity about him.

I noticed that his hair sat heavily on his head and he smelled stale, a combination of fading Old Spice and a long day of meetings. A wrinkled shirt was unbecoming of a candidate with a serious intent, I thought. He might have noticed my discomfort, and with little left to say, he asked, "Will you vote for me?"

I couldn't tell him no and I couldn't lie. I kept my promises, and I wouldn't make one I didn't intend to keep. Instead, I answered his question with a question. "Will you sign my place card?"

I think he got my point.

"Sure," he said, as he signed the small place card made out of green construction paper with my name on it. Flipping it over, he wrote in ballpoint ink, "To Terry, from Dick Nixon."

Wayne returned just as Nixon disappeared into the gathering crowd.

My three months in Baltimore passed quickly, and my psychiatric rotation ended. I had arrived in Maryland as a young girl filled with the promise of a blossoming life and left as a young woman who had come of age. Wayne and I continued dating and eventually he proposed, putting a diamond ring on my left hand. I accepted it and wore it with all the promise a future life with him might bring, but time and distance didn't help our relationship. He didn't understand my needs. It was simple: I wanted a plan. I wanted somewhere to live with a sense of place. He didn't understand that. I had already lived with uncertainty, and I wasn't ready to carry that feeling into my future. While I thought he was listening, he never heard me. We were engaged for about a year before breaking up and going our seperate ways.

Later in life, Wayne told me from time to time he would call places in Rumford to ask about me. He knew I had remained in my hometown. As an adult, Wayne would write the book *Laughing and Loving with Autism*, a personal account of his journey with his son. Wayne would also start Future Horizons, an important organization dedicated to providing education and resources about autism.

Years later in 2001, Wayne and I planned to meet again. He invited me to have lunch with him at New York's World Trade Center, near where he was going to give a presentation. The date planned for our lunch was September 11. Our plans, of course, were changed when the world changed. Terrorists attacked New York City that very morning. Wayne died in 2016 following his own battle with cancer. We never did meet again.

I graduated from nursing school in the spring of 1966. Thirty-three women dressed in starched white nursing uniforms marched to the front of the chapel at Cheverus High School in Portland to accept our diplomas. I had completed the three years of study required to become a registered nurse and was near the top of my class. I felt a sense of accomplishment having completed the first part of my life goal.

During the fifties and sixties, a woman's role was limited in a number of ways. Some women were able to transcend time and circumstance and be who they were, no matter what century they found themselves. I found my place in nursing, despite all of the indoctrination and guilt imposed upon me by Catholic teachings. I still wanted something more, something different. I wasn't sure yet what that would be.

Eleven

Rumford Community Hospital

I was twenty-one when I returned home to work. I lived with my mother. I was ready to repay my scholarship debt and take my licensing exams. The scholarship award program guaranteed a steady parade of young graduate nurses would come every year to work at Rumford Community Hospital. Previously, it had been challenging to lure young nurses from a city hospital to a small-town hospital. The scholarship idea solved that problem, and I was grateful for it. In return, I would work there for one full year.

I also applied to serve as a nurse ambassador on the SS *Hope*, a hospital ship operated by Project HOPE. The vessel, originally a US Navy hospital ship called the USS *Consolation,* was donated to Project HOPE in 1958. Under this new name, she served from 1960 until 1974, when she was retired. It was a job I really wanted, as a lingering dream of mine was to serve as a nurse on the hospital ship offering services throughout Southeast Asia, the same regions that Dr. Dooley had served.

One day not too long after, a letter arrived for me from Project HOPE. In my excitement, I ripped it open, but all my anticipation drained away when I saw the first word: "Unfortunately." The organization only accepted nurses with a minimum of two years of clinical experience to serve on board the hospital ship. I had to wait—and work—until then.

"What's the matter, Terry?" my mother asked.

She could tell from my body language that the letter had upset me. My tears and disappointment were comforted by a mother's understanding. Two years felt like an eternity.

My first day of work at the small community hospital was the next day, and I didn't sleep well the night before. I'd wanted to be a nurse for as long as I could remember, and now I was. My uniform sat starched, ironed, and ready. The thin black velvet ribbon on my nurse's cap was perfectly positioned, and my school pin identified the nursing school I'd attended. A name tag with the letters "RN" after my name completed the picture.

Nurse Terry RN was ready for action.

My first assignment was on a medical-surgical unit where I would work the three-to-eleven evening shift. Seasoned nurses would teach me the nuances of the art of nursing and I would get the kind of hands-on experience every nurse needs during their first year out of school.

There were many differences between a big city hospital and a small rural one. Some differences were subtle; others were not. In the city, nurses and doctors were available for consultations, opinions, and help. In these outlying rural hospitals, there were often no doctors actually present in the entire hospital. They were "on call," but they weren't physically present. They had their own private practies, often in their homes or in nearby small office buildings. At Rumford, nurses were the backbone of the institution. A keen sense of observation and curiosity was a necessity. In the entire staffing pool, there was only one male nurse. He had served as a medic in the Army. Of fourteen physicians, there was only one woman. It was commonly thought in those days that women didn't have the temperament or the brains to become physicians.

The Rumford hospital had a more relaxed idea of professional behavior than the Catholic city hospital I'd come from. Everyone here was called by their first name.

"Please call me Marilee," the head nurse said. "We are a small hospital and work closely together, so we are all on a first-name basis."

I appreciated the informality. Marilee had been in charge of this unit for more than thirty years. What she said was law. I would learn chain of command from her. It was also the busiest unit in the hospital, with phones ringing, buzzers buzzing, and an overhead paging system barking out commands at full volume. It was exhilarating, as I was in the middle of all of it. I liked the energy and believed my experience with Marilee would be good for my career.

"This is a very busy unit," Marilee continued. "We can only be effective if we know our patients and each other. Take the clipboard with the data sheet, Terry, and visit every patient on the unit, check their vitals, including temperature and blood pressure. Move along as quickly as you can because we have a lot to do today."

I was ready for the task. The "cart" would come along with me. It was a small white metal cart with four wheels that always squeaked, heralding my arrival. It carried all the tools of the trade—a blood pressure cuff, sterile gauze for dressing changes, thermometers, and everything else that might be used during the evaluation process.

As I stood at the door ready to visit my first patient, I took a moment to remember what it had taken to get me to this threshold. Lots of late nights of study, lack of sleep, and selfless hours of care for patients had shaped my ideas and my education. Fulfilling my dreams of becoming a nurse started here. I adjusted my cap, tightened the belt of my uniform, straightened the seams on my white nylons, and stepped into a semi-private room to see my first patient. I was ready for this, but my confidence level was still living in a shallow pool.

"Hi, Mr. Daigle" was my entry-level greeting.

He had heard the squeaky wheels of the cart coming down the hallway and spotted me as I appeared at his bedside, completely dressed in white. I must have looked like an apparition! Without my asking, he lifted the bedsheet to show me his abdomen, covered with sutures that crisscrossed his belly. In a most professional and empathetic gesture, I touched his arm reassuringly. Touch was considered an essential part of good nursing care.

"Looks great, Mr. Daigle. No sign of infection here," I said, as I proceeded to take his temperature and check his blood pressure and catheter before moving on.

"Is there anything you need right now?" I asked.

"Yes," he said. "The pain is killing me. Can you get me something stronger than those candy-coated pills they pass off as painkillers?"

I read his chart and saw that he hadn't complained to anyone about his pain before—or if he had, it hadn't been documented.

"Let me see what I can do," I said.

At the nurses' station, I found Marilee and asked, "Does Mr. Daigle have anything else for pain?"

"Give Dr. Royal a call and see if he would be willing to order something more effective," she shouted out as she hurriedly moved away from me down the hallway.

Dr. Albert Royal was the most influential physician in the hospital and the most feared. He was on every committee and served as the liaison between the paper mill and the hospital. His uncle had founded the hospital during the early days when the paper mill was being built. In this small town, the hospital and the paper mill had a symbiotic relationship. The paper mill couldn't exist without the hospital, and the hospital couldn't survive without the paper mill. After medical school, Dr. Royal returned here to do exactly what I was doing—repay a debt.

For a brief moment, I felt a kinship to him as I dialed his office number. His office nurse interrogated me.

"Can't this wait until Dr. Royal makes evening rounds?" she asked impatiently.

"I don't think Dr. Royal would like having his patient in pain for that long," I answered.

"Fine," she said. Her tone made clear it was anything but.

After a short wait, Dr. Royal came on the phone, his voice gruff. He clearly was in no mood for interruptions, and I was interrupting. He knew that I was one of the new scholarship nurses.

I told him about Mr. Daigle's discomfort.

"Oh! That old bastard. He always wants something," said Dr. Royal. "Take him out into the field and shoot him."

He hung up.

I just stood there, flabbergasted. Had I heard him correctly? And if so, what was I supposed to do? When Marilee returned to the nurses' station, I told her about my conversation with Dr. Royal, and she laughed.

"Terry, he knows you're one of the new nurses starting out this week," she said. "That's just his way of testing you. He's a big tease and likes to catch the new nurses and get away with it. Trust me, right now, he's taking it easy on you. Once you're not the new girl anymore, you'll really be in trouble."

Marilee knew how to handle Royal. There were coffee-shop rumors about a past romance, and I had certainly noticed meaningful looks and friendly touches between them.

For my part, I didn't think Dr. Royal's "joke" about shooting the patient was funny. In my youthful view, it was unprofessional, and I didn't appreciate this type of humor. Eventually, though, Dr. Royal seemed to take a shine to me. And I, in turn, started to feel like I was learning how to handle him and the other doctors.

The situation with Dr. Royal reminded me of the time during my surgical rotation in nursing school when I was assigned to the urology service. My first experience in the operating room was a surgical case on a seventy-year-old man scheduled for a circumcision. An advanced age for a circumcision, no doubt, but it was on the schedule and my name was assigned to it. It wasn't my place to ask any questions beyond that. The patient was prepped in the standard way, with a surgical scrub to the area and a shave. A circumcision sheet with a center opening was draped over him.

I was informed by the two physicians preparing for surgery that my nursing role in this case was a very important one. As a second-year student in awe of surgical surroundings, I paid absolute attention to what they were saying, not daring to look at them or, worse, the patient's johnson. The physician emphasized the importance of holding the shaft of the patient's penis with a firm grasp and remaining absolutely still. He grabbed the patient himself to demonstrate.

"Now, Miss B., hold this man's equipment with your right hand in place, like this. The success of the surgery depends on it, and we're counting on you."

Then both surgeons left the operating room, saying they would be right back.

I stood there alone and afraid to move. I was left with a sleeping patient, holding his penis in a firm grasp, as I had been instructed. They had convinced me they were depending on my steady hand for good surgical results. I did what I was told, waiting for them to return to the operating suite.

When I felt his penis begin to firm up, I looked around the room in a growing panic.

Through the small window in the operating room that faced the hall, I saw the faces of the two physicians, laughing because I had fallen for their prank.

I had been forewarned about their operating-room antics, but I hadn't been prepared for them to prank me.

"I don't think this is funny!" I yelled when they came back into the surgical suite.

"We're sorry," they both said as they proceeded with the surgery in an amused state.

If I had told on them, it would have gone like wildfire throughout the school. I decided to keep it to myself, but it was the kind of game-playing student nurses were subjected to on a daily basis. I got an A for the rotation and earned the reputation of being a good sport, but I still didn't care for their idea of humor.

Dr. Royal came in for evening rounds, apologizing and laughing that his comments had upset me. Marilee must have told him. He ordered stronger pain medication for Mr. Daigle, and I had my first official shift as a registered nurse under my belt.

Twelve

A Mainer in Paris

I met Lilly in the hospital cafeteria. Like me, she was a scholarship nurse. Although we were classmates at Stephens High School, Lilly and I hadn't shared any classes and hardly knew one another. Now, though, we found ourselves at the same hospital as newly graduated nurses, both working the three-to-eleven shift. We started taking our dinner hour together.

"Have you made any plans for next year?" Lilly asked me one evening.

We were both obligated to work a full year to repay our scholarship debt, and I was committed to the obligation, but given the opportunity to study music and art, I would have. The nursing scholarship gave me a profession I could rely on, and I took it. But I had a wanderlust that only grew stronger as I got older.

"I'm going to travel," I said, surprising myself. I spent a lot of time thinking about seeing the world, but it was the first time I'd said it to someone else. I liked the way it sounded. Saying it made it feel like more of a possibility, like something that could actually happen.

"Where will you go?"

"Europe," I said casually, as if I had already mapped the whole trip out and bought the tickets.

"Would you want someone to travel with?" It was obvious that Lilly said this without thinking.

"Sure," I said, not really expecting Lilly to follow through and not wanting to hurt her feelings.

But it turned out that like me, Lilly had no plan after her scholarship debt was repaid, and the more we talked about it, the more I realized I really didn't want to travel alone. We started planning our trip together.

We were helped along by a newly published book called *Europe on 5 Dollars a Day*. Arthur Frommer's book was originally written for American GIs living in Europe, but a growing number of young Americans wanting a taste of European travel would catapult the book to bestseller status. Most overnight lodging listed in the book cost less than two dollars, including breakfast.

A loosely organized plan would take us to Dublin, London, Paris, Madrid, Barcelona, Nice, the Riviera, Cannes, Vallauris, Rome, Florence, Salzburg, Munich, Frankfurt, and then back to Paris. We had no agenda, no real itinerary, no reservations, and no car. We would travel by plane, bus, train, and foot with the freedom to go wherever each day took us. We planned to visit as many museums as we could and do it all on five dollars a day.

It was the late sixties, a time of perceived safety for travel, a freedom to live life, and the opportunity for adventure. As I said my good-byes, Dr. Royal asked if I would be coming back.

"Of course," I said, and I was off.

I was still twenty-one when I arrived in Paris in the fall of 1967. Visiting the City of Light wrapped me in youthful euphoria.

Color, lights, and a cacophony of sound overloaded my senses. I was a long, long way from Maine in just about every sense, although there were things that felt familiar. The poetic sounds of the French language were implanted in my brain during childhood. My grandparents emigrated from Canada in 1916 and brought the language with them. Although they spoke French with their children, the language was largely lost by my generation. In Paris, I listened to people talk, intent on hearing a few familiar phrases I might recognize.

We'd already been to Ireland and England and had some practice in keeping within our budget of five dollars a day when we arrived in Paris. We walked everywhere, climbing stairs and trotting along on pathways of cobblestone to visit Montmartre, Sacré-Coeur, and the Eiffel Tower. We visited as many French bakeries as our budget would allow. I bought a silk scarf and a French beret from a vendor on the Left Bank of the Seine and wore them with my Levi's, which were the most essential part of my wardrobe, with the just-broken-in feeling that made them perfect for wearing days at a time.

On the streets of Paris, we heard music playing from somewhere and everywhere throughout the city. Long days were spent at the Louvre, Notre Dame, and Les Tuileries. Versailles trumped them all. The palace, with its gold magnificence, lush gardens, fountains, and lavish landscapes, galvanized my interest in French culture and history.

In Paris, I found a new independence of spirit, a coming of age. Not only did I feel different, I viewed myself differently as well. I was beginning to understand just how large the world really was, and I was ready to see more of it.

After spending two weeks basking in the magnificence of Paris, we activated our Eurail Passes and headed to the next stop on our journey—Madrid, Spain. It was the first trip by rail for both Lilly and me.

As the old train rumbled up into the Pyrenees Mountains, the nighttime temperatures dropped and it grew cold. No one warned us about this, and the train compartments were not heated. The locals had a simple, elegant solution: They wrapped themselves in newsprint, which did a remarkable job of holding in body heat. Some of them shared their papers with us, and these makeshift blankets kept us warm enough that we even managed to get some sleep.

The Hotel Macarena was our destination in Madrid. At the reception desk, we were greeted by the host and brought to see our room before registering, as was European custom. No one would stay in a hotel in Europe without inspecting the room first. Our room was bright and sunny, with twin beds and colorful drapes. We had a gorgeous view, overlooking busy city streets and amazing architecture. After two weeks in London and two weeks in Paris, we were more seasoned travelers and understood the necessity to stretch every dollar. The Macarena offered a prix-fixe rate, including breakfast and dinner, making it a real bargain.

On the night of our arrival, we were served a family-style meal at ten in the evening at a long farmhouse table set for twelve. Most residents were aging permanent guests who chose to retire there and live out their time enjoying the service and comfort of a small hotel.

At dinner that first night, we met Oscar, an older gay man with no family. The hotel was his home, and the parade of guests functioned as family for him. He immediately liked both Lilly and me, affectionately referring to us as "brats." He spoke English very well. We were the youngest guests at the table and the only Americans. The other dinner guests were curious about our lives and our reasons for visiting Spain. After a month of anonymity and living along the edge of other people's lives, we were excited to stand at the center of attention.

As young American tourists, we were ignorant of the realities of life under the repressive regime of Gen. Francisco Franco. However, we soon learned that just because we knew nothing about it, didn't mean it wouldn't affect us. Under Franco, who ruled Spain as a dictator from 1939 to 1975, Spanish women lost their identities and ambitions and were forced back into the confines of the home, making motherhood their primary social function. Women were not allowed to wear pants in public, a rule that I wasn't aware of. As I walked throughout the city in my Levi's, I was threatened in Spanish and called *puta*. I was pushed and yelled at, but I spoke no Spanish so I didn't understand why.

Oscar cautioned I might be arrested and thrown into prison. It was bad enough I was a woman wearing pants in public, but it was even worse that I was a woman walking along the streets of Madrid wearing pants *and* I was unescourted. The freedoms we enjoyed as American citizens didn't transfer here. Oscar continued to give advice and warnings, asking questions every night at dinner about our plans for the next day.

In the middle of the first week in Madrid, another American named Bill arrived during dinner. He carried a Martin guitar and projected a boyish presence. Bill won the opportunity to study the flamenco style of music with the master, Andrés Segovia. As a student of music myself, I was excited about Bill's opportunity to learn from the virtuoso classical guitarist. Noting my enthusiasm, he invited me to attend one of his lessons. Lilly wasn't interested, which was fine. By this time we'd realized we often didn't share the same interests and had no problem doing things independently of each other.

Segovia's studio was a rectangular room darkened by heavy maroon silk drapes with tassels. Once my eyes became accustomed to the semi-darkness, I recognized the maestro sitting at the far end of the room. It was a dramatic setting, and he sat patiently waiting for his student. He was clearly irritated by my presence, and although he nodded politely, he asked me to stay in the waiting room adjacent to the main studio. I listened to Segovia play cadences of the flamenco style of guitar as Bill followed, replicating the notes with expertise.

When the lesson was over we returned to the hotel, where he left his guitar, and Lilly joined us as we walked to the Plaza de Toros. We were going to a bullfight.

As we entered through the main gate of the stadium, we found it filled to capacity. The crowd cheered for both the bull and the bullfighter. Beer was sold in the grandstand by the cupful, and as the afternoon wore on, the crowd drank more beer and became more animated. When the bullfighter killed the bull, the crowd went wild.

The significance of bulls in the Iberian Peninsula dates back to the Paleolithic era. In 1879, the rediscovery of the Altamira caves in Northern Spain revealed stunningly detailed paintings of bulls from an estimated fourteen thousand years ago. Almost a century prior to this discovery, renowned Spanish artist Francisco de Goya began transferring bullfighting scenes onto canvas, completing several works between the late eighteenth and early nineteenth century. His colossal artistic strength elevated the event as a national symbol while highlighting the complexities of its practice.

I liked the work of Goya and viewed his connection to the matador and the bull at the Prado Museum, but I didn't appreciate the violent and bloody culture of Spain or the oppressive nature of its government. It was exactly opposite the romance of Versailles and the freedoms of Paris. Although there were many things that I loved about Madrid, it was Paris that taught me the essence of *joie de vivre*.

Across the street from our hotel was The Caves, an old thieves' den repurposed into a bar and nightspot. We spent almost every night there after dinner, meeting others our own age, sitting around and talking at century-old wooden tables. By candlelight, leaning against walls carved out of ancient rock, we sat until the wee hours of the morning, sharing opinions and our youthful view of life as we knew it. We spoke softly and intimately as single words became poetic phrases. I felt relevant in conversations and became more animated as we drank sangria, ate tapas and fried sardines, and embraced the magic of Madrid.

From the back of motorbikes skirting in and around the city, I saw a city sleeping with all of its lights on. I became a part of the population of people who sat on benches in museums and spent leisurely hours enjoying vast collections of art and history.

When it was time to leave Madrid, I left in sadness. Of the three months spent in Europe that summer, Madrid and Paris forever remained ensconced in my memory.

As we were leaving, Bill walked us to the train station, promising to see us back home. We never did meet again.

Thirteen

Back to Rumford

Returning home after three months overseas was a letdown. Yes, I found comfort in family and in the stability and beauty of Maine's Western Mountains, but the trade-off was a sense of isolation within the granite circle. I had tasted the excitement and independence of life overseas and wanted more. I found freedom in city living, and enjoyed an anonymity that small towns cannot offer—particularly in small towns where you grew up. Big dreams don't come easy in tiny spaces.

While Lilly moved on to Boston to work in a city hospital, I returned to Rumford with a promotion and a new assignment. Dr. Royal, now in charge of the entire medical staff, was pleased to see me return. "We missed you while you were away, Terry," he said.

After my trip to Europe, Dr. Royal and I became closer at work, and at some point, I was surprised to realize he was fast becoming a friend. I was a good nurse, and he knew he could count on me to care for his patients with respect and competence. Although I was restless, I loved my life at this moment. It was playing out as I had planned.

In the nurses' lounge around this time, I heard a lot of gossip about a doctor everyone simply called Doc. I hadn't met him yet. He had six children and was struggling through the end stages of a nasty divorce. Some nurses felt he was getting what he deserved, while others weren't sure they knew the full story. It didn't matter much to me either way. All such talk, at that point in my life, was just break-room gossip.

When I finally met Edward "Doc" Martin, I was twenty-two and still naive. I found myself drawn to him as a curiosity, and suddenly, the questions of what actually happened during his first marriage—and who was to blame for what—grew more interesting and personal.

Doc was charming and possessed an utterly unshakable confidence. I hadn't met anyone like that before. Plus, there was no denying he was handsome. Even though he was nearly forty, he looked ten years younger, and although he wasn't tall, he carried himself in a way that made him seem as though he was. He had hazel eyes and dressed like he'd just stepped out of an L.L.Bean catalog.

His cocky attitude was the signature stamp of his personality. Some didn't appreciate his earthy, frank sense of humor, but that never stopped him from saying whatever he thought the moment called for. He could be crude, but a plain, direct approach to conversation made him accessible to anyone. If you were a friend, he would be your friend for life. Some nurses called him Dr. Kildare, after the title character of the popular television series. The new heartthrob physician had a reputation and a roving eye, too.

By the beginning of the year, I was assigned to the emergency room as the charge nurse on the evening shift. Doc came by one night and formally introduced himself. As a solo practitioner with an outside medical office, he used the ER in the evening to see patients after his regular office hours. Almost from the start, when he needed help he asked for me.

On the evening Doc introduced himself, Dr. Royal quickly pulled me aside.

"Watch out for him," Royal warned. "He's been asking questions about you. In my opinion, he's trouble waiting to happen."

I didn't understand Royal's concerns or his warning, but I got the message. Royal didn't like Doc. I, however, had formed a different opinion—my interactions with Doc had been both respectful and professional, and his patients loved him.

One night, a distraught mother arrived in the emergency room with her ten-year-old son. Both were covered with the boy's blood, and she was holding most of the kid's nose in a wet handkerchief. The little guy had a pet raccoon, and despite everyone's warnings, he had let the animal out of its cage to pet it like a cat. The raccoon hissed once, and when the boy ignored this warning, the animal bit off the full end of the boy's nose, exposing two open nasal cavities. It was frightening and gruesome. Both the boy and the mother were in a state of panic.

Doc was the only physician in the hospital at the time, and he dashed to the emergency room. Ideally, the boy would have been transported immediately to the larger hospital in Lewiston, where they could do more for him. But before that could happen, he needed attention. Lewiston was too far to drive with the boy's blood squirting out sideways.

Technically, Doc wasn't a surgeon, but in the late sixties a small-town general practitioner had to be prepared for any circumstance. The boy was lucky Doc was on call. Doc's combination of confidence and curiosity made him well suited to the moment.

Whenever he'd had an opportunity to scrub in on a surgical procedure, he'd taken it. Life-and-death decisions didn't fluster him in the least. He was as assured as a person could be and as skilled with a scalpel and suture as anyone other than a seasoned surgeon.

"Set up the large surgical kit, Terry," he said in a commanding way as he pointed to the larger of the sterile kits sitting on the shelf in the emergency room.

I hurriedly set up the operating field, opening the sterile drapes to reveal instruments he could use to cut and suture. I prepared Novocain to inject into the raw parts of the damaged tissue surrounding the nose, and Doc applied pressure to stop the bleeding. Once the tissue was frozen, the boy didn't feel any more pain and quieted down.

Doc had a favorite brand of surgical glove, and when I opened the sterile package containing them, he gave me a nod of approval. When his hand slid slickly down into the glove, we had a moment. It was unexpected and didn't last long—just a nod and a smile—but it definitely felt intimate. Something happened in that split second that made me aware of the feelings I had for him. It took my breath away.

Doc focused his attention on the boy, stopped the bleeding, and reconnected the odd piece of the boy's nose. It all happened so quickly and calmly that it hardly seemed extraordinary, but it was. I saw Doc in an entirely different light afterward, convincing myself Dr. Royal had misjudged him.

We followed the boy's recovery every day in the emergency room for a week. A fine nylon suture healed the graft and he had a fully functioning nose, with only a hairline scar. The boy's parents gave the raccoon its freedom, exchanging it for a tricolor cat, and I had a new hero.

After that, Doc started hanging out in the emergency room in the evening and our conversations began to move beyond medicine. On one of those nights, he arrived with a stack of medical records. Before computerization, it took hours to handwrite everything in black ink.

"It's quiet here in the evening," he said as he sat down at the desk in the nurses' station. "I think I'll work from here."

When he finished writing his medical records, he said, "Have dinner with me tomorrow night."

It wasn't a question but rather a statement. Somewhere in my mind, I answered no, but my head and my mouth didn't seem connected, and what came out was, "Yes."

Truthfully, I was flattered by the invitation and curious about Doc. What would be the harm in having dinner with him, I asked myself. Dr. Royal's warning was a seed planted in my head and remained a nagging thought, but Royal didn't like Doc and Doc didn't like Royal, so it was a wash, I thought.

The next morning, I told my mother about my dinner invitation.

"I hope you said no," she commented.

"I said yes. What's the harm in having dinner with him?"

"Plenty!" And she left it at that.

I stood at the threshold of starting my own life, and my mother instinctively felt I was no match for Doc. I was young and attractive. He was divorced and alone.

When Doc and I started dating, some people said he was too old for me and they had a case! He was nearly twice my age. Still I found him attractive in spite of that age difference, or maybe because of it.

My mother didn't know Doc, but she had read about him in the newspaper and formed an opinion from the headlines about his divorce. A man with an ex-wife, six children, and a busy medical practice was not what she wanted for her daughter. She had survived her own divorce and it hadn't been easy. She didn't like the idea that history might repeat itself. I had convinced myself it wouldn't.

Fourteen

Doc

Who was this man everyone called Doc? Edward "Doc" Martin had been a precocious child, recognized early on for his quick wit and intellectual capacity. He was a local boy who grew up in Mexico, just across the river from Rumford, and graduated from Mexico High School in 1945. He was always at the top of his class and it was assumed he would accomplish unusual things in his lifetime. No one held this opinion with more conviction than his doting mother. And the two of them shared a lot in common. Irish by ethnicity, temper, and looks, she, too, had been at the top of her class, graduating as valedictorian from the same high school as her son. She was loyal to a fault and would bestow that attribute on her eldest son.

His curiosity wasn't only directed toward intellectual pursuits. He was curious about all manner of things.

"Stop it," Dora, his classmate, yelled during morning recess.

In the second grade, he attempted to see what was under her brightly colored school dress. She told this story at every class reunion and blushed each time she repeated it. The word "stop" meant nothing to him.

When he was of the mind to learn more about whatever he was researching, he also wouldn't be stopped. By ten years of age, he was already a force to be reckoned with. Good grades, good looks, and a "go after what you want" attitude eventually led him to some of the best schools on the East Coast. Without a family pedigree or money to back him, he was encouraged by his professors. Bright, cocky, and motivated, he was unmistakably exceptional, and his professors recognized ability when they saw it.

To some degree he was also naive, always believing it was ultimately human nature to do the right thing. He didn't include himself in that estimation, of course.

Rules didn't matter to him and "compromise" wasn't a word he used. Things must be the way he wanted. He could lead, but he wasn't interested in, nor did he seek, the structure of a team. He merely expected people to follow him, and if they didn't, he would forge ahead himself. It was the curse of being exceptional and narcissistic.

There seemed to be nothing he didn't have a talent for. By the age of fifteen he earned his pilots license and once, as a teenager, flew a Piper Cab under both the Memorial Bridge and the Morrison Bridge in Rumford.

Doc once told me he wanted to be a writer, and he wrote several history texts in his spare time. He was offered a football scholarship to Colby College, but by the end of his second year, World War II was raging and there was a mounting interest in patriotism and a need for young recruits. Doc enlisted in the Navy in 1945, wanting to be a fighter pilot. He was stationed at Pearl Harbor, and once made an impression by winning a boxing match against a man who would become the world middleweight champion in the fifties. His dream of being a fighter pilot ended when the war ended, although not before he "stole" a fighter plane from the base. He flew it around until he ran out of gas, knowing he would spend time in the brig no matter how long he flew.

After his service ended, Doc returned home to finish his education. At the end of his junior year at Colby, he caught the eye of the Dean who was aware of Maine's need for family doctors. He made arrangements for Doc to interview with William Bingham at the Bingham Foundation in Bethel, Maine. Everyone at Colby was impressed with Doc, and so was Mr. Bingham. As Doc sat across from his desk, Bingham picked up the phone to call the University of Vermont. An interview with the Dean of the medical school was arranged for that very week. Doc was admitted to Vermont with most of his tuition covered. The mandate was that he return to Maine and practice medicine, the same traditon most of the graduates followed.

In Rumford, being a local boy gave him a long view of the town's history and the perspective to connect dots like no one else. Some considered him a trailblazer and an agent of long-overdue change. Others saw him as a disagreeable, disruptive man.

Doc's family and the family of his first wife never got along, and ultimately, neither did they. After thirteen years, six children, and extensive emotional damage, their marriage ended. The town, ever conservative, looked unfavorably on their divorce, which in turn hurt Doc's standing in the medical community.

It seemed everything was made difficult by their divorce. Cousins became enemies. Family members realigned themselves and their loyalties. Doc's children grew rebellious. Battle lines were drawn. It all got complicated and was never actually resolved. The breakup of the family was permanent, and they moved forward, accepting their own dysfunction as normal.

Fifteen

Town Without Pity

During the fifties and sixties, a doctor's reputation was linked to his lifestyle. Personal standards were key to keeping the respect of peers and patients alike. A nice house, a faithful wife, accomplished children who attended prestigious colleges—these were all part of the identity of a small-town physician. In small towns like Rumford, folks stuck their noses in everyone's business, and the doctor's business was at the top of their list.

Doc's splashy divorce put him on the wrong side of the fence with the conservative physicians at the hospital. In addition, he had too many new ideas and opinions that didn't sit well with the outdated cast of characters that made up the hospital staff. His divorce gave them a good excuse to ostracize and isolate him. Kind and gentlemanly physicians from another era, they no longer were curious or willing to grow with the times.

When I returned from Europe, marriage was the furthest thing from my mind. I relished my newfound freedom and confidence and wanted to take full advantage of both. But conversations at work between Doc and me led to a friendship, which led to dating, which meant I, too, became part of the daily gossip in the break room. It wasn't in my best interest professionally or personally to date him, but once we became intimate, I was captured.

Intimacy and sex are powerful tools, and he used them on me. My inexperience and naiveté worked to his advantage. For example, when he told me he was sterile I believed him. He said his ex-wife had convinced him to have a vasectomy, which, he said, meant there was nothing for us to worry about when having sex.

It was a lie.

Suddenly, I was pregnant.

Shocked and in disbelief, I got tested to be sure. I used an anonymous name on the test requisition and waited a long, agonizing week for the results. When the test came back positive, all doubt was erased—I was pregnant. I felt as though the life I imagined for myself was being ripped away.

I couldn't wrap my head around it. It made no sense.

"How is this possible?" I asked Doc. "If you had a vasectomy, how could I be pregnant?"

"Terry, I never told you I had a vasectomy," he said, impossibly, nonsensically.

I knew very well what I had heard him say. After six children and several miscarriages, his ex-wife was done, and after a lengthy discussion, he decided to have the procedure.

"I did it for her," he'd told me, as if he should be canonized for such an act of self-sacrifice.

I believed his denial over what I'd heard him say earlier, with my own ears—what I knew he'd told me. There's a term for what he was doing—gaslighting. And it worked exactly as he intended: I believed him and doubted myself.

Looking back, I realize, of course, he knew he hadn't been sterilized. In knowing that, why would he risk getting me pregnant?

There was only one reason. He needed me and getting me pregnant would make it difficult, if not impossible, for me to get away.

I was raised in a fatherless household and spent most of my youth wondering what it might have been like to have a father in my own life. I remember the night he left us and the emotional damage it caused. Was I going to do to my unborn child the same thing that was done to me? I cried, night after night, wondering what I should do. Even through my panic, I realized neither abortion nor adoption were options for me. Abortion was illegal, and I would never give up my child.

There were also social considerations. Unmarried and pregnant in the sixties was complicated at best. It came with an unshakable aura of shame, finger pointing, and whispers. I told no one. I became quiet. I had wanted to be the main character in my own life story, but that character wasn't Hester Prynne of *The Scarlet Letter*.

My coworkers sensed something was going on. They asked a whole host of questions that I refused to answer. I needed time to think and to process, but time was running out. I was experiencing morning sickness, but still working. I started gaining weight and wore looser clothes to hide it. I knew I could only hide my pregnancy for so long. I felt abandoned and alone. Dealing with the hormonal changes and the dilemma of pregnancy occupied my every thought throughout the day. I dreamt of it at night. I woke up to panic attacks.

Finally, I told Doc the news.

"Let's wait and see how it comes along," he said. "Sometimes women abort naturally before the end of the first trimester."

I think he meant, in an inept way, to be comforting, to offer me the possibility of an out. But I didn't want an out. I wanted him to admit he'd lied to me. I wanted him, the father of my child, to be a different man than he was, to be someone I could trust and rely on. But what I wanted would prove to be the least of Doc's priorities.

By the end of my fourth month, my baby was moving and the morning sickness went away. I exchanged physical malaise for an ever deepening sense of shame and guilt. My belly was growing, and it wouldn't be long before wagging tongues would catch on.

I explored any idea that came to mind. I started looking for an apartment far from town. The baby was mine to keep, and I would have it, with or without Doc.

On a quiet and gloomy morning in late November, at the end of my fourth month of pregnancy, Doc came to me and said, "Let's get married."

He'd decided to claim the child as his own and while it wasn't perfect—wasn't even close to everything I wanted and needed from him—it was enough to tip the scales and help me decide. Not exactly the joyous occasion I'd imagined when I thought of getting married.

I said, "Yes."

We drove to Portland and met a justice of the peace in a tall brownstone building on Congress Street. He found a homeless woman standing outside his office to serve as a witness. Somewhere in the building, a beginner piano student was learning to play music from *La Traviata,* a story of a fallen woman who earns her redemption through sacrifice. The repetitious, meaningless notes both sound and sour were the unharmonious accompaniment to our vows. It seemed an ill omen.

When Doc slipped a thin gold band on my finger, it was done. There were no familiar faces or loved ones to share in the moment. There was no traditional wedding march and I didn't wear a fairytale wedding gown. There was nothing about this day that I wanted to remember, yet it was a day I could never forget.

The homeless woman signed the wedding certificate and the justice of the peace gave her twenty dollars. Like the betrayal by Judas, I felt as though I had been sold. Money had exchanged hands, and I would pay for my redemption through sacrifice. As the unknown witness put her hand out for money, she looked at both of us with a broad toothless grin, said, "Youse lucky bums!" and quickly disappeared.

I was twenty-two, pregnant, and newly married to a man who I knew had lied to me.

Sixteen

The Day After

The morning alarm ringing at seven was the first sound I heard when I awoke on the first day of my marriage. We were living in Doc's house in Mexico. There was no honeymoon—not even a few quiet days to settle into the enormity of what we'd done. I had quit my hospital job and was working for Doc. Office hours began at ten, and the telephone was already ringing for appointments.

"What's for breakfast?" Doc asked.

Whatever I had done, whatever I had accepted, began here, today. Just two days earlier, I was free, unmarried, pregnant, Catholic, and ashamed. On this day, I was married, pregnant, redeemed, and placed on a path toward social redemption. While there was some relief in that thought, it would cost me.

I had no idea just how much.

I called my mother, telling her I had gotten married.

"You made your bed, Terry," she told me. "Now you will have to lie in it."

And that was it. She hung up and I stood there listening to the dial tone.

Growing up in the fifties, I had an Ozzie and Harriet view of marriage and a childlike idea of what married life would look like. Because of my own parents' situation, I never really saw it up close in real time. I lived in and around Doc's life now, my own life not just subsumed but gone altogether, and the unspoken but ironclad expectation was that I would do whatever he told me and never forget my place.

What I didn't understand was that from the time I met Doc I was being groomed for the sexual appetite of an older man and was powerless against his exploitation. I was exactly what he needed. As a registered nurse, he knew that I could manage his medical office and care for his household, his kids, and him. I was a perfect fit for his needs, but my needs weren't the same as his. I had been on my way toward independence and discovery of self. We were headed in opposite directions.

Looking back, I believe he targeted me to bring order to his home and stabilize his life. Pregnant and captive, I had betrayed myself. I accepted everything.

"There are no bananas in the house, Terry!" Doc shouted at me one day, early in our marriage.

I looked at him like a deer staring into headlights. Startled by his shouting, I was unable to move or respond. "This is his problem, not mine," I thought, but that's where I was wrong—his problems were my problems now and I had better get to addressing them.

"Don't you know anything about raising kids?" Doc asked.

It was the first weekend that his kids were visiting, and there were no bananas for breakfast. At the time, his two older children were living with us while the other four lived with their mother in another town. On this day, all six were in the house and he demeaned me in front of them sitting at the breakfast table, staring back at me. I felt helpless, and I was.

Early on, I viewed his behavior as that of a man overworked, trying to reconcile the missteps he had taken in his life. I gave him a pass for his verbal abuse.

That morning, I went to the supermarket and filled a shopping cart with bananas. At the checkout, the woman looked at me as though I had two heads.

"Feeding monkeys?" she asked, thinking she was funny.

"Sort of," I answered.

I brought home bags of bananas and placed bunches of them in every room of the house. I guess it was childish, but with few tools in my emotional toolbox to deal with him, it was all I could do to make my point. I was trying to do the right thing, but in front of his children, he was tearing me down. Some might call it divorce guilt. Whatever it was, it was a pattern of behavior that never changed.

"I got the point, Terry." Doc said, when he noticed the house filled with bananas and fruit flies, but that was all he said.

I convinced myself, because I had to, that on the right day and at the right time, things would change, and he would become the loving partner I wanted. When my life with him became overwhelming, I placed my feelings of disappointment and pain in small, imaginary Pollyanna boxes in my head. I couldn't dismiss or ignore those feelings, but in the moment, I couldn't deal with them either.

It was the beginning of a life where fantasy became my only escape. Emotionally, I lived my life alone and exclusively in my head. For years. From the outside, I'm sure it looked grand, even like a fairy tale: Young nurse marries a handsome doctor, with all the prestige that brings in a small town. Moving into a home with children, a dog, and a busy medical practice might have sounded idyllic to some, and even a bit romantic, but it was not what it seemed, looking in or looking out.

Divorce was never a consideration. I understood the pain of it, from a child's perspective, all too well. Instead, we would all learn how to live with the consequences of staying together.

Seventeen

The Granite Bowl

We lived in what some called a Granite Bowl, thinking the mountains protected us—and maybe they did. But they also kept us trapped. The mountains that surrounded our town were covered with lush green forests and tributaries that flowed to merge with the Androscoggin River. I imagine at one time it must have been an idyllic place, Eden-like. But Eden had been plowed under and replaced by a rapacious and sprawling industrial complex that occupied most of the land in the valley and seized the eyes' attention away from what natural beauty remained.

In the struggle between industry and healthy, livable land, the balance always tipped in favor of industry. The geography of the area made it a bad location for a growing population and a polluting industry to coexist. Everything that came out of the stacks was held in by the mountains and eventually, inevitably fell back into the valley in one form or another. The stink, the noise, and the caustic air made life untenable for some, uncomfortable for all. But in a one-industry town, there's nowhere for a workforce to pivot. Even if you come to discover the work that feeds you may also be killing you, there's little choice but to keep doing it and hope you're one of the lucky ones who successfully tiptoes through the acid rain.

Or you deny what you know altogether.

Those who made paper and depended on the weekly paycheck used bluster to cover up what they suspected, what their bodies must have told them, at some level. "Breathe it in—it's the smell of money," the mill bosses would say, and the workers repeated the same phrase so often they believed it, too.

As the paper industry grew, it wasn't prepared for and didn't foresee a time when it would overtake the entire green space in the valley. Generations of folks had lived and worked there. The mill sprawled, the river turned dirty, and future planning was left to the future. Some recognized the need for the town to grow beyond the manufacture of paper. Tourism came up often in conversation as an option for growth. But tourists didn't come to our town—or if they did, they sure didn't stay long. Most often, they drove through as quickly as they could, with their windows shut tight and air conditioners turned off. Reasonable people, sensible people, people who didn't depend on paper for their livelihood, knew they didn't want to breathe whatever was responsible for that smell.

There were, and remain of course, plenty of faithful defenders of the paper mill who claimed they were used to the smell. By and large, we trusted and believed everything around us was safe. We were controlled by the paper mill, conditioned to be obedient by the Catholic Church, and taught to keep our mouths shut by our families. In many ways, it was an unholy trinity.

My baby girl was born the spring of 1969. Everything about her personified beauty and the magic of a new life. I nursed my newborn in our historic house directly across the river from the paper mill, so close I could hit it with a rock. My girl was pink and beautiful, with delicate hands and feet, even as our lives were filled with toxins—some we could see and some we couldn't.

The house we lived in was part of the early history of Mexico and had to be occupied by a practicing physician, a condition written into the will of the last owner. When it was offered to Doc, he bought it and moved in, hanging his shingle to practice general medicine in the same town where he was born. Only the river separated us from the mill.

After his divorce, Doc stayed in the house, and when we married, I moved in. While nursing my newborn, I always kept a suitcase packed and hidden under my bed. At twenty-three, immersed in the care of my baby, my new and confusing role as a wife and stepmother, and the responsibilities of a busy family medical practice, I felt ready to bolt half the time.

Even as we had our problems at home, Doc remained a dedicated and important public servant—the crusading town doctor. What worried him most early in his career was what still worried him now—the town's sky-high cancer rates.

Early on in our marriage, in the middle of an inescapably hot and humid night with an air inversion so intense there was hardly room to breathe, Doc sat bolt upright in bed.

"What's the matter?" I asked.

I thought something was urgently wrong. And, in a sense, something was.

Despite the fact that I had shut and locked all of the windows in the drafty old house, the pungent chemical odors that blanketed the area always seemed to be stronger in the middle of the night. I thought we were safer with the house closed up tight, but in fact, toxins linger longer and accumulate in more concentrated levels in airtight spaces.

"It's all connected," Doc said, sweat pouring from his forehead.

"What are you talking about?" I asked, still half asleep.

"Water, air, chemicals, unregulated dumping, cancer, disease—they're all connected!" he continued.

I still didn't really understand what he was saying, and when I finally did, it took me a while to become convinced he was right. Even though I'd seen the pollution in the river and smelled the chemicals in the air, there was a kind of mental block that kept me from being able to believe they were harmful. Like everyone else, I'd been conditioned to trust, not to question, and this conditioning was powerful.

Doc and I talked about the relationship between chemical contamination and the human body until the sun came up, and although we had no way of knowing it, on that night, our lives changed. It was the early seventies, and without realizing the magnitude of the problem, we had just stumbled onto the precipice of a crusade that would place us in the middle of a thirty-year controversy with the paper mill, the town, the state, and the local medical establishment.

Eighteen

Acadian Heritage

While toxic waste issues tied to the paper mill were bubbling to the surface, my personal life continued to move forward. I gave birth to two more children, which officially cemented my role as wife and mother. I finally unpacked my suitcase, accepting the reality that this life, while not what I had planned, was nonetheless the one I was going to live.

While we had our issues, one thing Doc and I did share was a love of history. We both had a direct relationship to the Acadian diaspora, which is how my Prince Edward Island family ended up in a small paper mill town. During the second Industrial Revolution, from 1850 to 1914, the curious and the hungry arrived in America from all over the world in search of work and a new life. In his 2011 book entitled *Introduction to American History* Brian R. Farmer puts it rather poetically:

> The emigrant brought with him something we do not see. He may have in his hands only a small bundle of clothing and enough money to pay his railroad fare but he is carrying a kind of baggage more valuable than

bundles or boxes or pockets full of silver or gold. It is the knowledge of customs and memories and a trade brought from the fatherland. He has already learned in his home country how to do the work at which he hopes to labor in America. In his native land he has been taught to obey the laws and to do his duty as a citizen. If this is true for the emigrant, then it is true for all of us.

Early attempts to establish fishing villages or create a center for trading furs on Prince Edward Island failed, and the French concentrated their colonizing efforts along the St. Lawrence River from Quebec to Montreal. Prince Edward Island floated magically on the waves of the Atlantic Ocean, and my ancestors floated along with it. Peaceful and content, the years passed as industrious early French settlers established their lives on majestic farmlands. The Micmac tribes called the island *Abegweit*, meaning "a peaceful place." For these early settlers, who worked hard, prayed hard, and subsisted on what their gardens would supply, the name held true. My ancestral grandmothers were strong women adept at farming and preserving their food for the long winter months, a skill the Micmac taught the French. Fields of wheat and potatoes were grown in the short growing season before the cold winter snows arrived to blanket their lives.

Mostly Catholic, the residents of Prince Edward Island were loyal to their beliefs and each other. They had deep trust in the guidance of the Church and were secure in that trust.

Today, if you travel these ancient pathways, you will find the most dominant feature on the landscape are the cathedral-like churches that dot the hills and valleys everywhere you look. It wasn't unusual for these large parishes to boast nine hundred families, and those families were big, as the priests encouraged every couple to have at least six children. They were good Catholics and they would obey.

My ancestral grandmothers survived on farms with dirt floors, without running water, and with corncobs stuffed between rafters to offer protection from temperatures that hovered below zero for months. They were creative with the few foods that were stored in their root cellars. Someone once told me how her grandmother could make meals with almost nothing, stretching one egg to create a soufflé that would feed all six of her children. If their children were lucky enough to go to school, they might walk the five or six miles on dusty, muddy, or snowy winding paths. If learning from books didn't interest them, they became farmhands. Those who stood out academically were encouraged to don the liturgical vestment of the priestly white alb or the long black dress of the nun. Life in the Church was a great honor and brought a sense of pride to any Catholic family.

My ancestors were isolated from the rest of the world by both geography and history. They would tell the story of the Acadian Deportation of 1755 from one generation to another, whispering its tragedy on front porches and at family gatherings. They told of the horror of English soldiers capturing farmland by stealing it. Great lessons were learned from this event, and it was so catastrophic that our family history became embedded in our genetic memory. My ancient grandmothers were uprooted from their homes and placed on ships that were unseaworthy and sent to the four corners of the world. English officers separated husbands from wives, mothers from daughters, and fathers from sons.

The fear that this could happen again was always at the forefront of my ancestors' minds as they kept their families close and known to each other. It was their only protection. They had survived that way once, and they could do it again if they needed to.

My family tells the story of Peter Bernard, who returned to Prince Edward Island after the English soldiers left. He found farms and crops burnt to the ground in a political strategy focused on getting rid of the French presence in the Maritime Provinces. Peter was sent to France on one of those unseaworthy ships but would later return from France to Prince Edward Island, his homeland. When he returned, he arrived in Tignish in the spring, and from Tignish, he walked sixty miles to Nail Pond, carrying an ax over his shoulder while his wife carried their one-year-old child. It is said that Peter cleared a spot in the woods overlooking the sea, where he built a log cabin. He managed to stay alive by fishing and snaring rabbits. Based on the climate and the landscape, this was clearly an achievement of courage.

Once it was believed that the English soldiers had truly left, some of these resilient farmers returned to see if their homes had survived the burning. They still feared the English soldiers, and it would forever be written in our genetic memory that forces at play that could destroy everything in a single evil moment of time. My ancestors rebuilt, but it was never the same.

Everything depended on the growing season. A rainy summer would guarantee a lean winter, and a lean winter would leave them facing a desperate spring. Many were tired of this insecurity. When word came from American cities that jobs were available for anyone who wanted to work and they could earn a weekly paycheck, there was a significant migration of the young. They left Prince Edward Island, the only home they had ever known, and traveled to America, often with no more than a loaf of bread and an extra pair of knitted socks.

Among them were my great-grandparents, who sold their farm and moved to Rumford in 1916.

Like my maternal grandparents, Doc's paternal grandparents came from Prince Edward Island and New Brunswick. They were born there, migrating to Rumford also around 1916, when the paper mill was new and in full working mode. Doc's mother was Irish, and although she married a man of Acadian ancestry, she had no love for the French or their customs. French was not a language she and her husband, whom we knew as Papa, shared, and certainly not one that she wanted to learn. Most Acadians were French Catholic. She was an Irish Protestant, and if it's true that opposites attract, it worked for them.

Papa had all of the characteristics typical of men of Acadian lineage. He was patient, loving, and kind, and he took good care of his family. He could fix most anything and was terrific company. Oral history became very important to our historic memory, and Papa recalled an old uncle who, in later years, afflicted with dementia, sat on the front porch in a chair that his own mother had rocked him in, cursing the English throughout the day. He couldn't remember his own name, but somewhere, buried deep in the recesses of his brain, what his family had endured remained. When speaking of the Acadian deportation, Papa would lower his voice and speak so quietly he almost couldn't be heard. He whispered what he knew of his own history as though he feared some kind of reprisal.

Doc learned his own history the same way the rest of us did—by word of mouth. That was enough, however, to make him seek out every history he could find, to read book after book on the Acadians and what became of them. Together, we started our own local group dedicated to Acadian history. Like our crusade against the paper industry, we felt this was also a search for justice, for answers to the secrets of a history we didn't understand.

By the end of the seventies, our research led us to France itself. We wanted to visit the ancient pathway our ancestral Acadian grandparents had followed. The journey brought us to a place called La Ligne, in the region of Poitou, a small community south of Paris.

Nostalgically, we wanted at least one of our children to walk the pathways with us. So, Jonathan accompanied us, while Rebecca and Frank, the baby, stayed in Maine with my mother. Doc's other six children stayed at home with their mother.

It was an emotional journey. The two-week visit provided us with the information we wanted to know and much more.

In fact, the trip inspired me to write a mixed-genre cookbook containing recipes and history celebrating the women of my Acadian culture. Their limited resources left no crawling creature or ocean denizen safe from their boiling pots, and this was reflected in their recipes. Their story was one that I wanted to capture.

My inspiration came from an unexpected event. During our visit to Paris, we connected with a group called *Les Amitiés Acadiennes*—Friends of the Acadians—a group founded in 1976 by Phillippe Rossillon. They were hosting a celebration dinner in a historic castle, and we were invited. As the only Americans of Acadian ancestry present, they sat us at the head table. It was quite an honor, but it came with an obligation.

"You must say a few words in French," Genevieve, one of the organizers of the event, told us.

I turned to Doc and raised my eyebrows.

"Don't look at me," he said. "I don't speak French."

The problem was that what little French I did speak was a patois, a blend of Canadian and American words and, at most, a scruffy first cousin to the Parisian version of the language. The true Parisian would choose words that reflected an elevated form of the language. My American version was a bit too country for this sophisticated crowd.

I can still feel my heart pounding when I think about that night. After the introduction, I stood and looked out at a sea of unfamiliar and curious faces. They looked back at me with anticipation, thinking that I might say something brilliant about how grateful I was to be in their presence.

Finally, I blurted out: "It's wonderful to be here tonight among your smiling faces!"

The entire room gasped. And then, silence. I had no idea why. But clearly something had gone wrong.

The problem, I would find out later, lay in my choice of words. A Parisian French speaker, when saying "face," would use the word *visage*. But the Canadian patois word was, simply, "face." Which sounds an awful lot like the French word *fesse*. Which translates into English as "ass." I had just told them I was delighted to be there amongst their smiling asses!

Fortunately, Genevieve came to my rescue, saying, "*MarieTh*érèse*, on ne serve jamais du mot, 'belle face,' c'est toujours 'belle visage.'*"

The confusion was cleared up, but nothing could be done about my embarrassment.

Nineteen

Office Gossip

"I don't like living on Main Street," I confessed to Doc one day. I'd grown up on the "lucky side" of town, an area that only occasionally got dumped on by air inversions and toxic emissions. After getting married and moving into Doc's house in Mexico, which was closer to the mill, I was directly in the dump zone and that provided me with a whole new perspective on the scope of the paper mill's pollution. Before my children were allowed to play outdoors, I washed everything with a water hose. I draped blue tarps over everything in the yard as protection from the black sooty particulate matter that never seemed to stop falling.

Doc didn't like it either, so we started looking for a house outside the perimeter of town.

In the seventies, Sen. Muskie finalized the most important environmental laws of the twentieth century. After helping father the sixties environmental movement, his work culminated in the passage of the Clean Air Act of 1970 and the Clean Water Act of 1972. Despite these federal laws, our local and state governments were not doing anything to protect people living in the river valley from the polluted environment. As had been the case for decades, the town fathers knew without the good-paying jobs provided by the paper mill there would be no local economy. The paper mill provided a living wage for the whole town, and in exchange, the paper industry as a whole was given carte blanche, its influence in state politics seemingly unmatched. It was the very definition of a devil's bargain.

Nothing has really changed since then despite changes in mill ownership. The mill had been sold to Ethyl Corp. in 1967 and would be sold to Boise Cascade in 1976.

One of my first forays into public policy regarding the environment was a meeting at the State Capitol in the eighties, where concerns about pollution in and around Rumford were being heard. I attended the meeting with a group of young mothers concerned about the unexplained yet undeniable rise in cancer and asthma in our community. We sat with our brown bag lunches, watching as a fleet of industry attorneys walked single file into the room, outfitted in power suits and carrying briefcases overflowing with documents favorable to their argument that the paper industry's use and disposal of chemicals was safe and legal. It seemed to me a show of brute force meant to intimidate, and the message couldn't have been clearer: If the people of Rumford wanted jobs, then residents would have to endure chemical contamination. It was that simple. There was no room for compromise.

In the end, no one wanted to fix or limit anything. Industry was booming. Like a lot of mill towns, we were making a lot of paper, paying a lot of taxes, and buying a lot of cars. What kind of fool would want to throw a wrench into that kind of shared prosperity? Less celebrated was another boom at children's hospitals from

Maine to Louisiana, which overflowed with kids from paper mill towns suffering from rare and deadly diseases.

In the years to come our river valley would earn a new nickname—Cancer Valley.

Where we lived—in our historic house, where poison fell from the sky day and night—we could see and hear the heartbeat of an industry that never slept. The noise and activity were ceaseless. Trains delivered chemicals, trucks delivered wood, and smokestacks delivered particulate debris around the clock. Looking for a house outside the valley became my priority. Most mill bosses—the same men who told us we had nothing to worry about, the same men who insisted the stench of the mill was "the smell of money"— lived outside the fallout zone. We would get out, too.

On the other hand, not everyone could leave, and some didn't even want to. There were plenty of residents who were content to remain in place, bring home a paycheck, buy a small weekend cabin in the woods, and breathe in fetid, foul, and poisonous air Monday through Friday. One problem was that too little was known about the cumulative effects of environmental pollutants in air, water, soil, and food.

But Doc, ever curious, had started to connect the dots.

When I first started working with Doc, our office was located in our home and in certain ways it functioned much like an old-fashioned general store. The office was a place of business, sure, but also a place for people to gather and trade stories and gossip. Doc encouraged this kind of scuttlebutt. Along with documenting the physical condition of every patient, he also made notations about things that piqued his curiosity—word about the best fishing spots, say, or a rumor that one of his patients had gotten himself into financial trouble. Of course, Doc also heard and made note of goings-on at the paper mill. Whenever there was a chemical leak or an injury, talk of those incidents would circle around town and ultimately be discussed in our office.

In the novel *A Tale of Two Cities*, Charles Dickens creates a character named Madame Defarge, a woman who knits in a pattern that reveals a list, naming the enemies of the people whom the French Revolution would destroy. Her wine shop was the hub of revolutionary activity. Doc found a similar niche of his own, listening to patients' stories and including them in the medical charts. What started out as an anecdotal storytelling exercise, the compulsive recording of a man with boundless curiosity, transformed over time into a written documentary.

There seemed to be no shortage of information about everything going on in the town or at the paper mill. Some of the local physicians, either tied to or working for the paper company, were placed in positions that created a conflict of interest. A worker knew if he was injured on the job, his injury could be listed in the column as "other" instead of more properly attributed to the dangers of mill work. When it came to some of the doctors who had professional ties to the mill, we believed their loyalty was to management, not laborers. After all, the mill itself had to be protected. Days lost for accidents were the thing they most wanted to avoid, and when they did occur, selective documentation helped to smooth things over.

Another cause for concern in Doc's eyes were frequent unreported accidental toxic gas releases. Since the mill was part of a self-reporting industry, most accidental releases went unrecorded. If word managed to get out anyway and someone came asking why there was no report at the time, the bosses would say the releases were too small to report.

Given what his patients were telling him, Doc smelled a rat. He brought his concerns to Dr. Royal. Doc and Dr. Royal never saw eye to eye on anything, and this issue was no exception. My marriage to Doc only made their relationship worse. Dr. Royal and I no longer spoke. Doc forbade it.

At the mill, if a worker complained of shortness of breath or dizziness after an accidental chemical release, they would be sent to first aid, where blame could be attributed to something else, like pneumonia or a flu-like syndrome. The worker would be instructed to take the rest of the day off, and that was the end of it. Fear and guilt were pervasive in a community and a workplace where someone was always looking over your shoulder. The workers had to keep their mouths shut and not be perceived as troublemakers, lest they lose their job.

However, workers knew they could trust Doc, and some were brave enough to tell him the truth.

One such man was named George. In the mid-eighties George had been diagnosed with terminal cancer. With death hovering over him, he no longer needed to keep secrets for mill bosses. He told Doc he'd been instructed to dump mercury into a large hole dug near the river. George didn't want to do it, but his boss told him if he didn't want to do it, they'd find someone man enough who would. George, who had a wife and six kids, was in no financial position to make a stink and risk his job. For the good of his family, he felt he had no choice but to do exactly as he was told. The incident George discussed was hardly the first time. George also confessed to Doc that he opened valves to discharge toxic chemicals into the Androscoggin.

I sat as a silent witness as George continued to tell the story about his boss. A voyeur of sorts, the boss was not willing to do anything illegal himself, but had the power to make someone else do it.

"He stood over me, watching to make sure I did it," George said, his shoulders slumped with shame and illness. Raised as a good Catholic, George knew the value of confession, and Doc was a good listener.

I witnessed every statement made by our patients. Our medical office became the place where evidence accrued and the truth became clear. Our hometown—as well as those down-river—were being assaulted by industrial waste in our water, land, and air. We believed mill management not only knew about it, they were ordering it to be done.

Doc became a voice for those who couldn't, or wouldn't, speak out. As these stories accumulated and the scope of the problem became clear, Doc decided he must sound the alarm.

Twenty

Multiple Contamination Principle

Question: Which of these chemicals was I exposed to just because I lived near the mill?

Dioxin, chloroform, ammonia, formaldehyde, carbon monoxide, nitrogen oxide, nitrates, ethanol, benzene, volatile organic compounds, nitrogen dioxide, sulfur dioxide, carbon dioxide, elemental chlorine, chlorine gas, hydrogen chloride, hydrogen fluoride, cadmium, diesel, gasoline, hydrocarbons, new source fuel or chipped tires, coal, and mercury.

Answer: All of them, of course.

Many studies are done on individual chemicals that are toxic or carcinogenic, but there's little data about the effect of a cocktail mixture like the one I, and others, had been exposed to every day of our lives.

How would you calculate the possibility of injury from the combined effect of these chemicals on the body? How could you gauge the seriousness of your own exposure? Probably impossible! But it seems reasonable to assume that if any one of these substances can by itself cause cancer or lung disease, then they would not somehow be magically rendered harmless when combined.

There were plenty of symptoms of multiple contamination exposure hiding in plain sight. Yet the industry was safe from responsibility and liability, as there was no way to demonstrate cause and effect.

Like us when we lived in Mexico, our neighbor Emily lived facing the paper mill, under the same cloud of particulate matter that showered us every day. Emily was petite and delicate, borderline frail even when healthy. She walked into our medical office one sunny morning without an appointment. Her husband was with her, and he was worried.

"Can Doc see Emily now?" he asked me. "I finally convinced her to see a doctor, but she would only agree to see Doc."

"What's going on?" I asked.

"She's been coughing for three months and hasn't had much energy for the past six."

Of course Doc would see Emily! He knew her and her entire family. Regardless, three months of coughing and six months of relentless fatigue, here in Cancer Valley, warranted an immediate examination. We knew the symptoms all too well, we heard a litany of the same thing over and over again.

Doc listened carefully to Emily's lungs, then passed the stethoscope to me. I heard it too. Muted breath sounds, wheezing, struggling, and lungs failing to fill with air. We knew Emily was in trouble. Doc and I exchanged glances. Experience taught us that this wouldn't have a good outcome.

A chest X-ray confirmed what we feared—Emily, age thirty-three, had a large tumor aggressively filling every available space in her lungs, pushing out good tissue. Not wanting to waste time, Doc referred Emily to a large medical center in Portland. She would undergo surgery, months of painful treatment, lose all of her hair, and become covered with black and blue marks from needles looking for a good vein. She would turn into a ghost of the woman she had once been. We would watch it all happen, again, and we would, again, do what we could—which is to say, not much.

Emily's was another version of the same tragic story and one that we dealt with every day. It was always the same. Families were forced to deal with rare diseases and cancer along with the complications of heartbreak and loss, followed by an early death. It was difficult to watch.

As we moved toward the end of the seventies and into the eighties, things were happening in our town that needed attention. Getting that attention would take more than one dedicated general practice physician and a nurse crying foul. Despite all of the letters Doc wrote in the seventies to town officials, legislators, senators, governors, lobbyists, medical associations, and newspapers, no one had any answers and no one seemed inclined to seek them. Most didn't even bother to answer Doc's letters. Rumford officials certainly didn't want to hear any of his concerns, and Doc's peers at the local hospital didn't seem interested, either. Our insistence that someone needed to listen and our repeatedly raising the issue in letters, at meetings, and in the local press won us no friends. We were becoming outcasts, Doc in particular.

The matter was complicated, of course. People needed to make a living, and the mill provided a good one, offering benefits, insurance, stability, and security. It represented the majority of the town's tax base. Mill scholarships were handed out at graduation, turkeys for Thanksgiving. Hats and shirts were offered as swag at the annual picnic, and folks wore them with pride, advertising for the company. The mill, as it had since the beginning, bought loyalty in many ways. If you worked there, loyalty was not just expected but demanded.

We felt the paper mill owned the town—everyone was trapped.

To be honest, misplaced loyalty wasn't the only thing at work here. Willful ignorance carried the day, too, permeating every aspect of our community. The mill was everything and everywhere. It seemed timeless, as though it existed long before any of us, an entity unto itself, almost conscious and self-aware. The chimneys, the walls, the trains coming and going, loading and unloading, the mountains of wood stacked like Egyptian pyramids—there was no escaping it. And most didn't want to, even if they could.

The granite circle of mountains held us all close. We knew everyone and what they were doing. Kids walked to school with neighborhood friends. Workers crossed swinging bridges that spanned the Androscoggin River, carrying metal lunchboxes bought at the local hardware store. They sat, year after year, eating lunch on benches and behind paper machines, swapping stories and lemon meringue pies for chocolate brownies. Runners ran, bikers biked, and walkers walked, breathing in particulates as they attempted to stay fit. Mothers pushed strollers. Shoppers went from store to store, spending their mill money.

Their lives were simple and straightforward, yet few fully grasped the idea that danger was involved in even the simplest things. Weekends centered around church activities and family gatherings. Few wondered aloud why benefits for families dealing with catastrophic illness were held seemingly every other week, even as they contributed some of their hard-earned mill money. All of our basic needs were met within the Granite Bowl, and like the feudalistic system of the Middle Ages, there was the common perception that we would be protected by the powerful and imposing Kingdom of Paper.

As it turned out, we weren't protected at all. We were used, poisoned, and, when necessary, discarded.

So, back to my original question: If every chemical on our list can cause harm, what happens when one compound mixes with another and another and still another? How would this toxic chemical cocktail affect our lives? What would a relentless wash of chemicals do to vulnerable human tissue as toxins were carried along the bloodstream from one fragile body part to another? Does body mass slow the distribution or enhance it, making children more vulnerable than adults?

Some considered limited exposure safe. Were they talking about a one-time exposure or the continuous accumulation that occurs year after year? Who would calculate the possibility of injury from one chemical or the cumulative effect of many chemicals?

No one was calculating or watching. And no one was answering any questions.

I'm neither surprised nor particularly dismayed that we couldn't count on the mill to protect us. More difficult to accept is the manner in which the Environmental Protection Agency ignored both our letter and the spirit of the Clean Air Act by leaving pulp mill emissions—highly toxic metals like mercury, organic pollutants like dioxins, and acid gases like hydrogen chloride and hydrogen fluoride—completely unregulated. What started in the 1970s when the EPA claimed it was *authorized*, but *not required*, to set limits for these uncontrolled pollutants was not resolved until 2021, when a District of Columbia Court of Appeals decided that the EPA has a mandatory duty under the Clean Air Act to address all toxic air pollutants. It didn't do much good for those of us who lived through the forty-plus years when the EPA had that duty but did not fulfill it. Earthjustice is a public interest environmental law organization that, according to its website, "wields the power of law and the strength of partnership to protect people's health and to preserve magnificent places and wildlife, to advance clean energy, and to combat climate change." Attorney James Pew, who represented Earthjustice in this endeavor, was quoted as saying, "The pollution from the mills is so bad that people living nearby can smell it and can get sick from the fumes, and the long-term effects of exposure on health can be even more serious. Communities living near pulp mills badly needed the protections that the Clean Air Act was intended to provide, and it is immoral that the EPA tried to shirk its duty to protect people from toxic air pollution."

But this is an abstraction. *Communities*, *protection*, and even *immoral* are ultimately bloodless, lifeless words. They don't reveal anything about the actual experience of watching one person after another get sick and often die, while you, the person charged with caring for their health, can do next to nothing to help.

Much more immediate and concrete, for example, was the morning the office phone rang, and Doc answered to hear Emily's husband on the other end.

"Hi, Doc," he said. "I wanted to let you know that Emily died this morning in Portland."

Here, then, are some facts that are not abstractions: At thirty-three years old, Emily died, quickly and painfully, of cancer. She left behind a husband and four school-age kids, who would have to find their way in the world without their mother's help and love.

We were right about all of it. Throughout the seventies, eighties, and nineties, Doc screamed from the rooftops and was viewed as the enemy by the mill and most who benefited from its business.

However, Doc was relentless and it was in his personality to never give up. Eventually, it wouldn't be enough for them to just ignore Doc.

Instead, they would start actively trying to shut him up.

Our hometown paper mill in June 1973. Photo courtesy of the U.S. National Archives

Twenty-One

A New Strategy

One day, in the early nineties, an environmental engineer from the mill called our medical office and invited Doc to dinner. The engineer said he wanted to discuss something with Doc. Doc was curious and agreed to go. I went along as his witness.

The engineer, a bright-eyed young man steeped in company philosophy and clearly on a mission, met us at the entrance of a local restaurant.

"Hi, Doc," he said. "So happy to have you here as well, Terry," he said, his gaze steady on me, assessing.

He led us to the best table in the restaurant overlooking the river. A waitress gave us their private wine list.

"Nothing but the best for you, Doc."

The engineer smiled, but the smile didn't touch his eyes. I was convinced Doc was being set up for something.

All through dinner, I waited for the engineer to reveal the real reason he'd asked Doc here. It was nothing but idle chat as we enjoyed hors d'oeuvres, appetizers, salads, and main courses.

Finally, over dessert, he stopped pretending to care how the fishing had been for Doc that summer and he got down to business.

"We want you to work for us," the engineer said.

"I wondered when you would get to the point," Doc replied.

"It would be advantageous for us to have a physician on board with your knowledge of chemicals and pollution."

It was no more or less than a bribe. They'd already demonstrated conclusively they had no interest whatsoever in what Doc knew about chemicals and pollution. What they wanted was to pay him in exchange for his silence and call it a job.

"Of course," the engineer said, "you would have to sign a nondisclosure agreement."

Of course, he would. And in doing so, he would become a toothless tiger.

"I'm not interested in being bought," Doc said.

The engineer was not giving up so easily.

"I can make this package really attractive for you, Doc," he said. "To start with, I'll double your salary."

The salary and benefits package were handsome, but Doc knew it was a bribe, and he turned it down for a second time. Dinner ended abruptly.

Although I agreed with Doc's decision, the truth is, the money they offered would have changed our lives. With our three children and sometimes the six children from Doc's first marriage, we occassionally had up to nine children to feed, care for, and educate. Although we agreed to care for his children every other weekend, during summer vacation, and on select holidays, I never quite knew who would be around. I cooked for twelve as a precaution. At the end of the 1980s, the mill money would have made things a lot easier for us.

But it was wrong, and we knew it. If we'd thought working for the mill would have actually resulted in changes to the papermaking process, we would have jumped at it. But we knew that wouldn't happen. Changes could have been implemented early on and would have saved our town from the consequences of rampant, unchecked pollution. It could have spared untold numbers of families the pain and expense of catastrophic illness. But changing the process of making paper wasn't cost-effective for the industry. And no matter what, money was always the priority and the bottom line. Leave well enough alone, many would say.

Although the price was high either way, we knew it would cost us much, much more to go along with it. It would have cost us our integrity.

Not long after this dinner meeting we started getting letters in the mail.

First came a notice from the Internal Revenue Service informing us we were being audited.

Another letter came from the Department of Human Services, saying they wanted to look at our Medicaid records.

And then Medicare said they wanted to review our charts and patient outcomes.

Someone had anonymously reported us to six different agencies, and all of these audits were going on simultaneously. We couldn't prove we were being targeted, but we knew we were.

One way or another, they would get Doc. The message was clear: If he couldn't be convinced to join them, they would destroy him instead.

"Cancer, cancer, cancer—is that all you can say? Why don't you leave well enough alone and mind your own business?" Doc and I heard many versions of this sentiment from board members of both the mill and the hospital. We heard it from town officials, fellow physicians, and neighbors.

There were conflicts of interest everywhere, and no one wanted to pay attention to issues affecting the bottom line. Everyone was making money, and wasn't that the point? Business was business, after all.

But Doc's business was his patients. They were sick and suffering needlessly, and he wouldn't just stand by and watch that happen without trying to do something about it—to make the people responsible accept that responsibility and change the way they did things. In the end, no one else was looking out for Doc's patients, not even the governmental entities charged specifically with doing so. The Environmental Protection Agency and the State Department of Environmental Protection continued to offer pretzel logic to excuse their inaction.

We were told air quality regulations are enforced to keep companies compliant, not to keep communities safe. Which sounds very official and sensible, until you ask yourself: What's the difference between the two? The answer is, there is no difference. Keeping companies compliant with the rules of the Clean Water and Clean Air Acts is precisely the same thing as keeping communities safe. Otherwise, what's the point of compliance?

From the large picture window of my living room, I had a clear view of two very large discharge pipes that continuously poured an unidentified brown liquid directly into the river. The discharge water was muddy and thick, and under the cover of night, valves were fully opened and more of the liquid was released when no one was watching. Like George's story, we heard other tales of mill workers being ordered to dispose of various chemicals and waste products. Even a child can understand that if you feel you have to do something in secret, chances are very good that what you're doing is wrong.

Runners check the weather before heading out for a long run. Hikers do the same. No one ever checks the level of pollution, particulates, air inversions, and ozone before taking part in activities that make you breathe faster and increase respirations.

Kids from both towns ran track, played football, and did other sports directly under the mighty stacks that polluted our valley. An elevated asthma rate among our children was just another thing chalked up to the cost of doing business.

In the seventies, the term "sacrifice zone" came into use to describe places where environmental degradation had permanently damaged the land. Like Detroit's 48217 zip code, Louisiana's Cancer Alley, and Houston's East End, Rumford was designated as a sacrifice zone. But whose sacrifice were we talking about? And who decided a sacrifice had to be made?

Were those being sacrificed and those who made the sacrifice experiencing the same thing?

Twenty-Two

Farrington Mountain

One beautiful day when we lived in Mexico, I gathered my two eldest children and took them across a small bridge over the Swift River that connects Mexico to Rumford. We were headed for Rumford's municipal skating rink. Olympic figure skater Dorothy Hamill had recently won a gold medal and the excitement created a resurgence of activity at the rink. What happened that day proved emblematic of the relationship between the two communities.

Mexico was the redheaded stepchild to Rumford's bright young boy. All the money from the mill—taxes and other financial benefits—stopped dead at the municipal boundary on that bridge. That was the reason we had to go to Rumford if we wanted to skate; Mexico couldn't afford its own rink. But when Rebecca, Jonathan, and I arrived, the rink manager told us that, as residents of Mexico, we weren't allowed to skate there.

"I'm sorry, Terry," he said apologetically. "If I made an exception for you, I'd have to do it for everyone."

Rules about poisoning people could be ignored, but rules about ice-skating had to be enforced. Surely, I could understand that!

We took off our skates and walked home, a place where pollution from the mill, of course, did not respect town lines.

I called the Mexico town manager and asked to be put on the selectmen's agenda the following week. Although the agenda was full, he was able to squeeze me in at the last minute. Doc decided to attend the meeting with me. Who knew that on this very night, we would witness one of the worst decisions our town's elected officials would ever make?

The centerpiece discussion at the meeting was whether to allow the mill to use Farrington Mountain, located at the outer edge of Mexico, as a landfill site. They wanted to use our town, not theirs, to bury whatever they couldn't burn. For an annual fee, the mill would be allowed to carry sludge across the river and dump it in a pit carved from the top of the mountain.

As it turned out, our selectmen were all too eager to go along with the idea. The senior selectman, who had held the position for many years, argued strenuously to allow the measure.

"Our town has never gotten anything from the mill," he said. "None of the tax money and benefits of making paper come here. Now they will!"

When it was pointed out that perhaps accepting massive amounts of toxic sludge was not a great idea for the health of the town, he brushed the concern aside.

"Don't worry," he said. "The mill executives have promised to take every precaution. They're lining the pit with Kevlar, and everyone knows that nothing can get through Kevlar."

Doc stood up and spoke.

"You can't allow this. Paper mill sludge has dioxin in it." he said. "And who puts a landfill at the top of a mountain? Everything you put in there will flow downward eventually."

It didn't register.

It seemed no one there could think beyond the handsome stipend promised by the paper mill. Time would prove Doc right, of course—the weight of the sludge would rip the Kevlar barrier and allow the chemicals to seep down into our wells and the river. But on this night, the selectmen deemed that impossibile—not worth worrying about. And dioxin: What the hell was that? From their perspective, Doc might as well have been a crazy person, ranting and raving in the street. They gave his objection the same amount of consideration, voting unanimously to approve the landfill.

Although many folks in the room that night were Doc's patients, and they respected him, they weren't able to see beyond the years they'd watched Rumford thrive and Mexico struggle to make ends meet. They didn't want to make the connection between sludge filled with dioxin and other highly dangerous chemicals and community health. The bottom line was Mexico didn't have much of a tax base, and the money paid by the paper mill to use the mountain would help.

Approve it and move on was the consensus. If you didn't know the word "dioxin" or what it meant for you and your family, that was of no consequence.

Yet.

And there still was no money for a skating rink.

Twenty-Three

Billy White Shoes

Rumford Community Hospital didn't employ a proper cardiologist. For years the board of directors had relied on the closest thing—a physician who, although not certified in cardiology, had taken a few courses in the discipline. He called himself a cardiologist, and the hospital was happy to do the same, given the prestige conveyed by having such a specialist at a small rural hospital. Never mind that it simply wasn't true.

The deception came to an end one cool evening when the doctor serving as Rumford's cardiologist rolled his tractor while mowing a slope on his lawn. According to local gossip, when they pulled the machine off of him, they found a bottle of Jack Daniel's still clutched in his hand.

That was how William Breesmen came into our lives. The board of directors, desperate to fill the cardiologist position, found him at a southern job fair. Breesmen, whom we nicknamed "Billy White Shoes," said he was a cardiologist, and the board was happy to take his word for it. In 1984, Billy rolled in to Rumford driving a candy-apple-red Mustang convertible that would turn out to be a rental, looking to all the world like a wealthy man pulling into a country club—silver-white hair, white linen suit, and of course, the shoes—white bucks with bright red soles. Billy knew the importance of a strong first impression.

The hospital sent out a mandatory-attendance memo for a meet-and-greet with the only doctor who had shown interest in the position of cardiologist at this little rural hospital, and the members of the board were on their best behavior.

At dinner I asked Doc, "Did you meet the new cardiologist today?"

"Yes," he said. "Strange guy."

"Strange how?" I asked.

"Hard to explain. Something about him isn't right."

"Did you look at his application?"

"Nope!" Doc said, scooping up more meatloaf. "He said all of his documents were on the way."

At that moment Doc was serving as chief of medicine and had a duty to vet new candidates. The chief position rotated among the medical staff, and it happened to be his turn.

"I don't have time for this shit," Doc said as he moved on to the apple pie. "I have enough work to do with my own practice. Running around collecting paperwork should be someone else's job, not mine."

The next day as Doc walked the halls of the hospital, he was greeted by a powerful and important board member, who grabbed him by the sleeve and pulled him into a side alcove.

"Take your time with this, Doc," he said in a low voice. "We need a cardiologist, so let this guy settle in before you have him filling out too many forms."

But the members of the board weren't the only people with power and leverage involved in recruiting Billy. Some local doctors also played a role. Some felt it would be financially beneficial to have a cardiologist for the hospital.

More than a month had passed when Doc found Billy, at the nurses' station in the ICU, enjoying the attentions of the nurses on duty. Sitting there with his feet on the desk and his chair tilted backwards, he was holding court, talking loudly about famous cardiologists he claimed to know.

Doc interrupted his performance.

"Got your application in order, Billy?"

"I'll let you know as soon as my documents arrive!" he said.

Billy flashed an annoyed smile at Doc. It was yet another red flag for Doc. How could someone be hired for a position at a hospital without any of the necessary documents. It was ludicrous. Doc was incredulous that Billy had been allowed to stay on staff for over a month without producing proof of his qualifications bordered on farcical.

Doc said he was reminded of the movie *The Great Impostor* about a man who pretends to be many things he's not, including a doctor. It crossed his mind he might be dealing with someone like that.

Doc was concerned about what he felt was a lack of scrutiny and he wasn't content to let Billy slide. As a hometown boy, Doc felt protective of the town, the hospital, and his profession. He wanted to complete the job he'd been assigned and be done with it, but that was proving to be next to impossible.

"Where are you staying?" Doc asked.

"At the motel in town," Billy answered.

Doc knew it well, as he passed by every night on his way home.

"Nice place," Doc continued. "When does your family arrive?"

"Just the wife and I, and I'm not sure when she will get here."

In point of fact, we were never really sure if Billy had a wife.
We certainly never made her acquaintance. And just as we would
never see her, Billy's supposed credentials never materialized,
either. We would have to accept on blind faith that he was a
board-certified cardiologist. A couple of mediocre confirmations
that he was actually a physician were the best we ever got.

Doc felt something was off. The pieces didn't fit, and his few
conversations with Billy's references hadn't been good.

Doc laid out his concerns to the board, but their need to
fill the position outweighed Doc's facts. They liked what they
thought Billy could do for them and took his word that he was
who he said he was. They advertised him as a board-certified
cardiologist.

Not long after the board approved Billy's appointment, one of
our regular patients, Marjorie, came into the office for her annual
physical.

"How do you like the new doctor?" she asked Doc.

"You know him?" Doc asked.

"Aside from seeing it blasted all over the newspapers, I work at
the motel where he's staying, and the entire housekeeping staff is
talking about him."

This was certainly interesting.

"What are they saying?" Doc asked.

"The first day he arrived," Marjorie said, "he had four banquet
tables brought to his room and lined up along the walls. Then he
took all these medical books from the back of his car and opened
them by category to specific parts of the heart placing them in
an order known only to him. He told me that if he needed to
reference anything, the books would be open to different cardiac
issues and readily available."

While Doc wasn't exactly surprised, he was alarmed. He kept listening.

"But that's not even the best part," Marjorie said. "He then ordered me to keep everyone out of his room. No maids, no cleaning, no fresh towels. Nothing! Just stay out and don't touch anything."

"Did you?" Doc asked.

"Of course not. It's my job to make sure that everything is okay in every room, so I had to peek in. Guess what he had under one of the tables?" Marjorie said, grinning.

"I'm almost afraid to ask," Doc said.

"Six pairs of white bucks, all lined up in a row. Counting those he has on, that's a clean pair for every day of the week!"

As I said before, there are no secrets in small towns. There are, however, plenty of people willing to pretend they don't know something's wrong when it's as plain as the nose on their face.

Twenty-Four

Doc Gets Sued

One of the promises often attributed to the Hippocratic Oath is "First, do no harm." Doc had been asked as chief of medicine to review Billy's credentials. None of his reviews were good, and Doc had found no evidence that he was actually a cardiologist. Although Billy said he was and this was printed by the newspapers, there was no real proof.

Doc reported his concerns to the chief executive of the hospital and the chairman of the board, saying it was a real problem for the safety of the hospital and its patients. A senior member of the board asked why Billy would say he was a cardiologist when, in fact, he wasn't.

A meeting of the Rumford Community Hospital's Joint Conference Committee, the most powerful body in the hospital, was called in May 1984. Made up of physicians and administrators, the committee's main purpose was to investigate and oversee sensitive issues involved in running the hospital. Confidentiality was expected, so issues of exposure or liability could be discussed openly and without fear. It was supposed to be a safety net for catching the truth.

It was a moment of truth for Doc. When faced with what he considered injustice, he felt compelled to step in and step up. He had faced the power of a polluting paper mill poisoning his patients and his neighbors in an ongoing battle. He had been discredited and labeled a whistleblower and now faced the same attacks at the hospital. He could just walk away and ignore the problem. Let someone else solve it—or not. But for Doc, exposing the truth was his only option. His social conscience compeled him to understand what was going on, and the responsibility of his position obligated him to shine a light on it.

"What about his status as a cardiologist?" an administrator on the committee asked.

"He doesn't have one," Doc said. "I called a hospital in Pennsylvania where he practiced."

"And what did they tell you?"

"That they wouldn't recommend Billy, as he did not handle critically ill patients. It was his opinion that Billy 'talked a better case than he could do.' He said Billy was not a cardiologist and probably had a personality disorder."

"Then what did you do?"

Doc said he called another hospital. That hospital told Doc that Billy applied for privileges in their cardiology department, and, when asked if he was board-certified, Billy answered in this way: "I took my examination not too long ago, and a funny thing happened. The fellow sitting next to me flunked his exam, and I passed mine, but they mixed the two up. So he got my score, and I got his. It's in the process of being remedied, and I'll bring you my certification as soon as they send it to me."

Billy was never able to provide proof as to his certification, to anyone. It didn't exist.

The difference was, at the hospital Doc called, Billy was denied cardiac unit privileges. At our hospital, the board of directors turned a blind eye and allowed Billy to continue practicing medicine in the intensive cardiac care unit and throughout the hospital.

In the days following the meeting, a deposition that took up the better part of a working day ended as sirens announced the arrival of an ambulance. An unconscious patient was brought to the emergency room. His wife arrived shortly thereafter in a panic and cried out, looking for her husband. They brought her into a room where he was being tended.

The patient was having a cardiac event.

His wife wanted the cardiologist who she'd been hearing about for months. Billy eventually arrived, but it soon seemed apparent to Doc that Billy was in over his head, inappropriately giving a beta-blocker to a patient who was barely holding on. Whatever chance this patient had to live disappeared with that injection.

The patient died. His wife filed a malpractice suit.

A wave of shock and gossip followed this event and spread throughout the hospital, taking up most of the conversational space in the break room. That death led to a general review of Billy's cases, in which several hundred patient charts were impounded and sealed by the court. In an out-of-court settlement, the widow was paid by the hospital's insurance company and she signed an agreement that obligated her never to speak of the award or the case.

Despite all of this, it wasn't over yet.

It was the summer of 1984 and, like every year, we escaped to our lake house on Ellis Pond, north of Rumford. We filled the car with kids, pets, and groceries and left for warm summer days with the sound of children laughing and playing along the beach. It was just far enough away from town, the hospital, and the intensity of a busy solo medical practice to offer us a slower pace. Not to mention, it was located outside the fallout zone of the mill. I looked forward to it every year and was content with the plaintive cry of the loon and the gentle, rhythmic, lapping of the waves at the edges of the lake.

This summer, though, the peace we'd come to rely on at the lake house was not had for long.

An early-morning phone call woke us. I heard it ring but ignored it. I gave a lot of my time and energy to the medical practice, but this was my vacation and I needed the break.

Doc answered. It was John, an emergency room physician and a friend.

"Have you seen the morning paper, Doc?" he asked.

"No," Doc answered. "I'm barely awake."

"You made the front page," John said.

"Read it to me," Doc said.

John quoted the headline exactly as it was written: LOCAL DOCTOR, HOSPITAL SUED FOR SEVENTEEN MILLION DOLLARS.

Forewarned by a member of the board of directors, who was alerted by the hospital attorneys, Doc knew something legal was afoot. No one had told him that the review had progressed to a lawsuit. The hospital had been identified as the deep pocket, and Doc had been named a defendant as chief of medicine.

I heard a sound in Doc's voice that alarmed me.

"What's going on?" I whispered to him.

All I got was an impatient hand signal that meant *Hold on, I'll tell you.*

Eventually, he hung up.

"Put on a fresh pot of coffee, Terry," he said. "John is on his way up with the newspaper. The hospital and I are being sued by Billy White Shoes."

Basically, Breesmen filed a lawsuit against Doc, the hospital, and one of the directors claiming defamation and intentional infliction of emotional stress following the meeting of the joint conference comittee. According to Breesmen, Doc made "defamatory and derogatory" statements about his character and his abilities and was out to get him. It all stemmed from what Doc had thought was a private meeting to discuss Breesmen's qualifications. According to Breesmen, Doc's comments had caused emotional distress and hurt him financially because of lost business.

I had long ago lost interest in the incompetence of those who were in charge of the hospital, but the lawsuit got my attention. The seventeen active physicians at the hospital were tasked with multiple responsibilities for the running of the hospital. Doc's service as chief of medicine was something he was obligated to do. It wasn't anything he wanted, and neither did I, but it was a rotation, and it was his turn. I resented it, as it took time away from our personal lives, and I'd asked him not to do it this time. He said he had to; it was his turn and his responsibility.

I'd listened, I'd heard, I'd understood. But now Doc was being punished for doing his duty.

Twenty-Five

Guilty!

After countless delays and years of litigation, a jury finally delivered its verdict shortly before Christmas in 1989—Guilty! Doc was found guilty of slandering Billy White Shoes.

However, the hospital was *not* held liable. Apparently, the jury viewed Billy White Shoes as the underdog and awarded him $3.5 million: $1 million for defamation, $1.5 million for emotional distress, and $1 million in punitive damages. In our view, members of the jury clearly ignored testimony by expert witnesses that Billy didn't know what he was doing. And they dismissed the fact that a hometown doctor was simply trying to do his due diligence to protect a community hospital and its patients. Instead, they believed that Doc acted with malice.

A nationally known cardiology expert, testified Doc had done the right thing. This expert stated that Billy had, in fact, attempted to take his boards in cardiology on three separate occasions, walking out of the exam room each time without ever completing them. After his third attempt, Billy was barred from ever taking them again. The jury seemed to ignore this part of the testimony.

Instead, the jury found Doc guilty of slander and further concluded that he acted on his own and out of malice. The hospital was released from responsibility. Doc was left to stand on his own.

When the guilty verdict was delivered, I felt the jurors just wanted to be done with it.

But we weren't done. We did have some recourse. Doc filed a motion for judgment not withstanding the verdict, or alternatively, a motion for a new trial. Basically, Doc filed an appeal claiming the verdict was excessive, not supported by the evidence, and was erroneous as a matter of law. The appeal would be decided by a judge, not a jury. As the lawsuits and appeals played out the very real fear that we could lose everything, including our home, was stressful.

In July 1990, Stephen L. Perkins, a superior court judge, issued his decision on Doc's motion. Perkins ruled that Billy failed to prove that Doc intentionally inflicted emotional stress, instead saying evidence showed that Doc's remarks at the meeting were "motivated by geniune concerns regarding patient care and Dr. Breesmen's professional qualifications."

Perkins also ruled that Billy did not present clear and convincing evidence to support malice, which would be required for punitive damages.

In the July ruling, Perkins granted Doc's motion for a new trial, unless Billy agreed to settle for one million dollars. The amount was the limit set by Doc's malpractice insurance and the amount tied to the defamation award.

After the judge's final ruling, Billy White Shoes, who had moved to Florida shortly after filing the lawsuit, essentially disappeared for good into the quiet of the night. After that last day in court, we never saw him again. I never knew where he went or what happened to him.

The judge's ruling proved only a partial victory. Yes, the award was reduced and we would not lose our home, but Doc's malpractice insurance carrier canceled him. Without this insurance, he was not allowed to work in the hospital and he never would again. In the aftermath of the verdict, Doc opened a walk-in clinic in the Rumford and Mexico area and saw some patients by calling on some doctor friends for help.

While Doc somehow coped with this injustice, internalizing it, I never got over it. I felt those who would defend the status quo at any cost won the day.

As we headed into the 1990s, insult was added to injury when Doc was diagnosed with an advanced case of prostate cancer.

We were certain of its cause.

Twenty-Six

Arsenic Cocktail

A story in the regional section of the morning newspaper detailed a double suicide. Everyone was talking about the shocking news at the coffee shop as they waited in a line that curled like a serpent all the way to the cash register. Long lines don't usually occur here, but today was different.

Julie, the coffee-shop barista, never missed a day's work, ever. She loved the gossipy aspect of her job and the front-row seat she occupied. Years of chain smoking had produced a gravelly deep pitch to her voice that allowed her to control the volume in any conversation.

I could hear her talking over the crowd.

"They were dead for three days before anyone found them," Julie announced, as if she had been given the scoop firsthand. "They were dressed like they had just been married. He wore a tux, and she was in a white linen dress with a veil."

When Julie spoke of the goings-on around town, most people listened close. That's because Julie got most of her news from Muriel, her best friend from high school. Muriel's son had been the sheriff in this county until he decided to take photos of what he thought were his finer attributes, showcasing everything he thought made him a "real" man. That was bad enough, but then he made the far worse mistake of posting the pictures on the Internet. There he was, naked from the waist down, wearing his sheriff's shirt, and badge. It took about two seconds for him to be identified, and it didn't end well.

Our town had had its share of adverse publicity, for sure, and it seemed nothing was too ridiculous to happen here.

Julie paused for dramatic effect, hitting the lever on the espresso machine. Steam hissed, and she practically had to shout to be heard.

"My cousin said the man was recently diagnosed with cancer that couldn't be cured, and his wife didn't want to live without him. They made a pact, wrote a note, and shared an arsenic cocktail. They died holding hands."

I'd read the newspaper article at home, so I knew about the suicide, but the version Julie told contained more sorrowful details than what had been published in the newspaper.

I grabbed my latte and left.

Doc and I knew the couple who committed suicide from our forays into the world of art and antiques. As friends, we had sat for hours in their quaint antiques shop, swapping stories about recent purchases. It was a part of the business that everyone engaged in and the part I loved best. Most everyone had a good story to tell, and whether it was made up or true, it was important to the provenance of any antique.

The unexpected deaths of our friends came as a shock. Over time, as his own cancer progressed, Doc became obsessed with what they'd done. He thought it was romantic for a woman to love a man enough to die with him.

One day, he asked me to die with him.

"It's like Romeo and Juliet," he said.

The first time he asked was over lunch.

"Are you kidding?" I asked. I really thought he was.

He wasn't kidding. Several weeks later he asked me again. The first time he'd sounded like he was just curious; this time, there was gravity to his question, as if my answer really was life or death.

"We could do the same thing, Terry," he said, as if suggesting a fun trip to a hot vacation spot. "We could die holding hands, just like they did. Don't you love me enough to die with me?"

He'd gotten nowhere trying to make the proposal sound appealing to me; now he was trying guilt. Perhaps he thought he could negotiate a deal. Clearly, he wasn't thinking straight. By this time the cancer had strengthened its grip, and he was starting to realize the end was approaching.

As he grew more desperate, I increasingly sensed real danger in his proposal.

I never truly considered saying yes, but at the same time I knew I had to keep Doc calm. I had lived with his rage for years and had become an expert at preventing and defusing it. While over the years Doc and I were truly of one mind when it came to our fight to protect the public health, our marital issues were always present. His cheating, verbal abuse, and controlling behavior created constant turmoil.

His most frequent threat to me during our marriage was: "If you don't do exactly what I tell you to do, there will be serious consequences."

At one point, he threatened to take our children to Australia if I didn't agree with whatever he wanted me to do. He would leave passport applications on the dining room table as a reminder. I honestly believed he would do it. I lived in this relentless cycle of abuse, oscillating between extreme "love bombing" followed by devaluation.

Asking me to die with him racheted my fear of him to a new level.

During this time, I thought long and hard about what kept us together. What makes a marriage last for three decades despite all the issues? One answer is that he was the father of my children; another, that he became my teacher and mentor. I learned a lot from him, and this knowledge opened my eyes to a world of interesting possibilities.

Looking back, I realize it was all a part of his mechanism of control over me. As willing as he was to teach and I was to learn, he would never go beyond a certain point. If he felt he was losing control—that I was learning too much for him to remain in absolute control—he would stop. Any idea I shared with him became his. That isn't to say that he didn't have creative ideas of his own, because he did. He just didn't want me to have any of my own.

He played psychological mind games that kept me staggering between self-doubt and uncertainty. When I wrote a cookbook after our visit to France, celebrating the women of my Acadian culture, Doc was displeased when the book brought attention to me. He couldn't abide my success, seeing it only as a threat to our life together.

"Writing your book was the worst thing I ever encouraged you to do," he said.

Truthfully, no one choses to be in an abusive relationship. Doc was kind to me in the beginning, and his kindness captured me.

And then there was pregnancy.

Many women would agree this is a game-changer. It was for me. Pregnancy was my first motivation for investing in a relationship in which my abuser wore a mask. Two more children followed. Placed in a glass house to nurture three children, I chose to stay. I was driven by fear, isolation, and complications involving the safety of my children, but I still had a choice, and I made it day after day.

My sister once said to me that she felt Doc systematically erased the person I was.

She was right, but at that point, he had isolated me, and I couldn't fully recognize it or do anything about it. I kept silent about the verbal abuse, emotional manipulation, and psychological torment. He counted on the fact that no one would believe me.

After all, how could anyone believe that this man, a cornerstone of the community, a beloved family physician who cared so much for his patients, who waged an imporant crusade against local polluiton, was hatching a double suicide plan? He was responsible for the health of so many as a doctor, had helped birth more than 2,500 babies, and was trusted implicitly. Asking any of those people to listen to the complex truth was tantamount to asking them to relinquish their trust and to disregard what they saw with their own eyes. I was the only one aware of the danger I was in. I felt I had no safe harbor and nowhere to go.

On some level, I had trouble believing it myself. Why would someone who professed to love me also want me dead? I had no visible scars from his abuse, just like the town had no visible scars from the paper mill. And like the paper mill, he would not be held accountable.

As I worked to maintain the status quo of our lives, the ground was shifting beneath my feet. In addition to all the reguar issues, I now had to deal with the fear that he was hatching a plan to kill me.

One afternoon in 2000 while he was resting, I drove to a pay phone at the general store a few miles down the road and dialed the hotline for abused women. I needed an unbiased view of my situation, and I feared he would hear me if I called them from home. I wanted an anonymous conversation during which I could lay out the facts and have someone tell me what I should do.

A woman with a pleasant voice answered my call. I told her my story and she listened attentively.

"Do you think I'm in real danger?" I asked.

I wanted the opinion of someone who didn't personally know Doc or I.

Her answer was swift.

"Get out immediately," she warned. "Tell me where you are, and I'll send someone to pick you up."

I thanked her but said I wasn't ready today. I needed time to process this.

"Don't wait too long," she cautioned. "You *are* in danger."

I lingered in the privacy of the telephone booth trying to understand my choices. On some level, I knew she was right, but my thinking was clouded. Still, those two stark words—"Get out"—were a powerful wake-up call. On one hand, it was comforting that an anonymous person on the other end of the telephone line believed me—believed what was happening to me was real. Yet I also knew Doc was dying, and it wasn't in my nature to leave anyone in such desperate need of help. I guess you can blame it on the Church and my years as a nurse.

Nothing made sense anymore. I successfully lived with Doc's manipulation for most of my adult life. As a master manipulator, he knew just how far to push me. He was always able to turn on the charm if he sensed I had leaving on my mind.

But this was a different time. He was facing death in the near future—and death was something beyond his control. He became more and more desperate and focused on what he *could* control—trying to take me with him.

I went to the market every Thursday. When I returned home one Thursday, the house was unusually quiet. There was a kind of eerie expectation that something was about to happen—or had already happened. I could see some furniture had been moved, which Doc wouldn't have been capable of in his weakened state. What was going on?

By now, at the end stage of his disease, cancer had infiltrated Doc's skeleton. Scans revealed bone lesions up and down his body. He slept in a hospital bed downstairs while I continued to sleep in our bed upstairs. Our former room together had become *my* room, and our bed was now mine alone.

I walked into my bedroom to hang my coat. It took several seconds for me to realize the room was almost empty. The old sea captain's bed crafted of bird's-eye maple was gone! Blankets and sheets were strewn about on the floor in the middle of the room.

After a few moments of pure bafflement, I realized this was real. What had happened in our house during the hour and a half I'd been gone?

I went back downstairs.

"What happened to our bed?" I asked.

Doc ignored me.

"Where is the bed?" I demanded.

"I sold it to an antique dealer," he said, as if that made perfect sense—as if I didn't actually need a place to sleep myself.

His face was expressionless.

"I told you no man would ever sleep with you in my bed. If you won't die with me, no one else will have you in my bed. Now I don't have to think about it anymore."

The cancer and his narcissistic personality now consumed him. He knew his time was limited and he would do everything he could to ensure his control over me, even after he was gone.

I was more afraid of him than I had ever been. I moved to another bedroom in the house with a lock on the door.

Without the marital bed in the picture, I hoped his idea of an double suicide had disappeared as well, but I knew this wasn't over yet. What he would plan next to take me with him wasn't clear, but I knew I would have to pay full attention to his every move.

As the cancer ate away at him, Doc slowly withered. In the final months, he weighed no more than ninety pounds and was more and more helpless. Every night, after I fed him and tucked him into bed, I went upstairs to my bedroom and locked the door to feel safe while I slept.

One night I awoke in the middle of the night and I could smell smoke.

"Oh my god," I thought. I opened the door to see smoke about halfway up the stairs. I quickly raced downstairs toward Doc's room to make sure he was safe. When I got to his room, the bed was empty.

I followed a trail of smoke through the house to the living room. He stood there stark naked. He had gathered some sticks and wood and started a fire in the middle of the room, not far from the fireplace.

"I was cold," he said. "I thought I would warm myself up."

One weekend night in late June 2001, our family ate one final dinner together. Everyone had moved away to live their lives. Some came home to see their father in his final days. Late in the evening, after everyone else had gone to bed, Doc was still awake and still thinking, still trying to figure out a way to control his fate. He went to his son sometime after midnight and asked him, "Do you think I can beat this?"

The answer was no. He was dead by morning.

Twenty-Seven

A Better Place

Rex Rhoades, editor of the *Sun Journal* in Lewiston, wrote an editorial after learning of Doc's death on June 2, 2001:

> In 1957, John F. Kennedy published *Profiles in Courage* and won the Pulitzer Prize for his biography. He told the stories of eight men of principle who stood by what they saw as the truth despite coercion and vilification by their peers. If JFK were alive today, I'd like to think he would have admired Dr. Edward Martin of Rumford.
>
> In the 1970s, Doc began speaking out about paper mills, pollution, and cancer. And for the next 30 years, he never stopped. Doc will be remembered as a tenacious adversary, the man who first dared to draw a direct line between the town's large paper mill and the deadly cancers he was treating.
>
> Life is full of mean little ironies, and Doc fell victim to one of them. He spent a good part of his career trying to warn his people, his community, about cancer. In the end, cancer got him too.

Doc will be remembered in many ways. He was the kind of doctor they don't make anymore. As the classic general practitioner, he would jump out of bed at night, grab his black bag and run to someone's house to care for a feverish child or a dying grandmother.

To many people, he was a loudmouth, a troublemaker, and a dangerous radical who dared to shake the economic pillars of his community. He spoke truth to power.

But did he win?

There's no doubt that the paper mills in our state are cleaner today than they were thirty years ago.

Medical science has dramatically affirmed Doc's point of view. The mill emits fewer toxins than it did thirty years ago, and the next 2,500 babies born in Rumford will grow up to enjoy cleaner air, cleaner water, and longer lives.

Is the world now a perfect place? No, and it never will be. Has cancer been defeated or pollution eliminated? Not yet. But is Rumford a better place because Dr. Edward Martin had the courage to stand alone? There is little doubt.

Twenty-Eight

Toxic Waste Women

During the year after Doc died, I believed there would finally be a reckoning for the paper mill. I was wrong. There wasn't. But I wasn't giving up.

There was still unfinished business.

One morning in 2002, after an overnight snowfall of about three inches, I watched as the mill pumped out particulates from most of its chimneys in variations of color and size from black to gray to white. The winds were swirling, and smoke was blowing in all directions around town.

Even though it was a miserable day, my friend, Ingrid Eriksson, and I decided we wanted photos of all this stuff. We headed out and traveled along the road next to the mill property. While I couldn't count the number of smokestacks blowing debris in the wind as one clouded over the other, one thing was for sure—the smell of money filled the air.

Ingrid was a doctor and part of a wider network of local physicians. Her practice was not in Rumford, but she saw patients in town on a rotating basis. She was also a strong environmentalist and we met when she had arrived on our doorstep one day, asking to speak to Doc. Although he was bedridden at the time, they spoke and I invited her to stay for dinner. She gladly accepted and became a regular Friday dinner guest. We shared lively conversations, often about mill issues. After Doc's death, Ingrid and I grew closer.

Ingrid did everything with a passion that was infectious, including being a founding member of our group. We didn't expect notice at a national level, but we could speak to what was occurring in our local communities. It was this aim that brought five like-minded women together. Initially, we called ourselves the Toxic Waste Women. Although there was some eye-rolling and even a sense of comedy associated with our chosen name, when we met, we were serious.

The five of us—Jenny Orr, Anne Morin, Shirley Damm, Ingrid, and myself—met weekly around an old wooden table in a small West Paris bakery where the coffee was good and the ginger snaps legendary. Shirley owned the coffee shop, and in the back room of the Hungry Hollow Country Store, we discussed the dire consequences of pollution and strategies to combat it.

We met week after week, attempting to enlist others to our cause. We opened our meetings to the public, but few people came. In 2003, there was seemingly nothing sexy about the cause and effect of pollution, and the idea that it could cause illness was still a somewhat remote concept. Despite that, we remained faithful to our weekly meetings and discussions. The five of us—a physician, a nurse, a neuroscientist, a chemist, and a baker—had an educated overview of Oxford County and its health issues. When our weekly discussions pivoted from raising awareness to figuring out what we could actually do about things, we ditched the name Toxic Waste Women and became Western Maine Citizens for Clean Air and Water (WMCCAW).

Outside, next to the uncovered digester, is a sign that reads, WEAR PROTECTIVE EYE GEAR. I opened the window to get a photo and was nearly blown out of the car. The smell of chemicals was overwhelming. Within a few minutes, I had a headache. I hadn't been to that part of town for some time, and it was worse than I remembered it.

At the same time, we saw students running on the old ball field, training for spring and summer sports. They ran, jumped, and, of course, they breathed, fast and deep, taking gulp after gulp of the toxic air.

The next day was Tuesday, and when the phone rang, it was Ingrid.

"Guess who called me today?" she asked.

"I give up," I answered. I heard the excitement in her voice and knew she had something important to tell me.

"The Common Ground Fair is putting together a panel of environmental activists. They want the us to do a presentation under the big tent at the Fair. It's a big deal, Terry."

"What did you tell them?" I asked, already knowing her answer.

"You know I said yes." She laughed.

As an orthopedic surgeon, Ingrid made tough decisions every day. This one was easy, because she was right—it *was* a big deal. The Maine Organic Farmers and Gardeners Association (MOFGA) puts on the Common Ground Fair, which is universally acknowledged as the biggest event of the year in Maine's agricultural community. The invitation and recognition would be important for our group. Helping to raise public awareness on issues of pollution was important, but bringing attention to the rising numbers of cancer and asthma rates was our first concern.

On the day we were to speak at the Common Ground Fair in 2003, we drove the one hundred miles in a car caravan full of computers, whiteboards, and fliers. Sharon Tisher, a lecturer who taught environmental law at the School of Economics and Honors at the University of Maine, presented first.

"Oxford County in Maine is in the worst ten percent of all counties nationally for particulates," she said. "'Particulate matter' is a term used to describe a mixture of solid particles and liquid droplets in the air. Defined by Mark Dawson, a local environmental code enforcement officer, 'They are a health concern because they easily reach the deepest recesses of the lungs and never come out.'"

Mead Paper Company was the only stationary source of particulates identified in Oxford County. At this point, the original paper company, Oxford Paper, had been sold to Boise Cascade and then to Mead Paper Company, passing the responsibility for toxic chemicals from one to the next. (The mill would be sold to NewPage in 2005, Catalyst Paper in 2015, and finally to Nine Dragons in 2018.)

While these sales were going on, fifty-three thousand people in Oxford County faced a cancer risk greater than one hundred times the goal set by the Clean Air Act. It was a shocking number. It was a call to action. We felt we were on the right track.

We were particularly concerned about the local impact of air quality regarding emissions from the Rumford mill, as it was in our backyard. It also had been named one of the state's top four air polluters in an Environmental Protection Agency inventory. Back in 2000, burning used tires as fuel provided a solution to the problem of tire disposal, while simultaneously creating another. Mead was permitted to burn up to ten tons of chipped tires per hour as a low-cost fuel, and we would breathe in the particulates that resulted. Our lungs were, in effect, dumping grounds for industry. Ours, of course, was not a new fight. Back in 1992, Doc had been appointed by the town manager of Rumford to be the municipal physician. Around this time, Boise Cascade had requested permission to increase the number of pollutants the plant would be allowed to release into the air. Doc opposed the increase, and in a letter to Dean Marriott, commissioner of the Department of Environmental Protection, he wrote:

> Because of our most unfavorable geographic location in a bowl-like valley, and considering the already high incidence of chronic respiratory and cancer illnesses in our town, our citizens cannot tolerate further water or air pollution. Paper mills should not be allowed to pollute the air of the towns where they are located by burning dioxin-laced sludge or used tires. They have apparently run out of places to bury the sludge, and now, under the guise of producing electricity, look for new ways to get rid of it, regardless of the impact on the health of the citizens of the community.

Doc's letter was ignored.

Now, a decade later, we found ourselves in the same place; only the players were different. It was now MeadWestvaco requesting an increase in their air emission permit. Nothing had changed.

Our group continued to target air-quality issues. We wrote a successful grant proposal and, with the funding we received, we were able to hire an environmental attorney. Our group formally challenged Mead when their Title V air emission permit came up for renewal again.

As part of our strategy, we began a house-to-house survey in the greater Rumford and Mexico area to study cancer rates among longtime residents living near the mill. We developed a newsletter and a website, seeking to attract the attention of state agencies mandated to protect the public. They had the resources and the power to make that happen, but there was little incentive for the industry to curb toxic emissions without citizen involvement. What we wanted from the paper industry was honesty and a willingness from individuals in the impact area to break the long-standing "code of silence" about the adverse health effects of this pollution.

At the Common Ground Fair, we took turns delivering fifteen-minute presentations. Ingrid, Anne, and Jenny went first.

When it was my turn, I opened my remarks with this introduction:

> I live in a town called Cancer Valley, where our water is contaminated, and our air is compromised as well. The name "Cancer Valley" was not awarded to us; we earned it on our own. In the center of my town is a tower which stands 412 feet tall. It's an emissions stack that burns a mixture of chipped tires (called "new source fuel"), paper mill sludge (which contains dioxin), and coal and wood waste.

It was obvious that I'd grabbed their attention.

Our group was happy to have had the chance to present at Common Ground Fair.

We soon learned there were other communities concerned with the effects of emissions. Living downwind from the paper mill, others outside the valley started finding their voices as well. But it wouldn't be the public officials or the politicians that we would hear from. Few politicians seemed to care about what was going on at the Rumford mill. No lobbyist, governor, senator, or representative came forward with any answers or interest in the concerns expressed by "we, the people." We were on our own.

In an attempt to quiet the noise and complaints coming from downriver, an environmental engineer for the mill said: "One would still expect the highest effects of chemical emissions from the mill to be seen in the immediate surrounding area." What he was saying was those folks living downwind had nothing to worry about, because the chemical emissions would mostly impact the area surrounding the mill.

It was *my* town and *my* valley that would capture these emissions. Although it was no comfort to those of us living in the polluted valley, it *was* an indirect admission of guilt.

In 1989, the EPA had published information about chloroform releases from the paper mill. In response to this report, the mill refuted the science by publishing in its newsletter, called the National Water Reuse Action Plan (WRAP) Sheet, this statement:

> We know of no scientifically credible data that would suggest that the employees of our mill or the residents of this community suffer from an abnormally high cancer rate from chloroform or any other substance associated with our facility. Therefore, we know of no reason for anyone to be alarmed at the reports associated with this highly questionable database.

Our town's most important employer and most powerful entity wanted everyone to know the EPA warnings were not something town residents should be concerned about. It was a bold and outrageous lie that many believed.

Did paper mill officials not know that in 1988, the dioxin-monitoring program designed to track toxic chemical contamination in fish was in progress?

Yes, they did know. The vice president of Boise Cascade at the time was quoted as saying, "Dioxin does not pose any real health risk, and any effort to require this industry to reduce dioxin is unnecessary due to the lack of a definite link between dioxin and cancer."

We believe this was another intentional lie.

When Ingrid spoke that day at the Common Ground Fair, she noted that the paper mill is a self-reporting industry. No one checks up on them, because they estimate numbers rather than measuring them exactly. The goal of WMCCAW, Shirley Damm told fairgoers, was to "test the air, water, and blood, relating chemicals to disease incidence. By monitoring, we can better understand what these chemicals are doing and try to decrease the amount of cancer."

While this was a good premise, without money for testing and with little public interest in learning the results, it would be an exercise in futility.

Sharon Tisher summed it up in her closing remarks: "For the twenty-five-year period from 1973 to 1999, across genders and for all types of cancer, Maine ranked seventh in the country."

She concluded by paraphrasing one of Maine's popular slogans: "This is not 'the way life should be.'"

Twenty-Nine

Looking Down the Barrel of a Gun

Jenny Orr and I decided we wanted to see the landfill site on Farrington Mountain, where the mill dumped tons of sludge into a Kevlar-lined pit. As part of our WMCCAW agenda, we were curious to see what was going on up there. They wouldn't give us permission to visit the site, and armed guards stood at every entrance. No one was allowed in.

It was around 2005, and at one of our weekly meetings a local man, Richard Bean, stood up and said, "I know how to get in there through the back gate. I used to hunt on top of the mountain but stopped when I found that the deer were full of tumors."

We took him up on his offer to show us the back entrance, known only to the few who used it for hunting. Richard was our guide and he warned us to be careful. Jenny and I were convinced that if we could get samples of the stuff reportedly oozing out of the ground, we might have enough evidence to stop the dumping.

We crawled under the fence and were on our way to the top of the mountain that had so captured our interest. It wasn't easy. The pathway was overgrown, and we had only a pocket compass to guide us. We saw many places where thick, iridescent, black ooze issued forth from the ground. We passed these smaller puddles, saving our few collection tubes for the mother lode.

What soured the moment—and ultimately, the day—was a guard looking our way and pointing a gun with a scope at us. He didn't see us, but I think he heard us. Attempting to hide, Jenny tripped and fell. She already had a bad hip and was due for surgery, and her fall—not to mention the presence of the armed guard—forced us to reconsider.

"Terry, I don't think I can go on," Jenny said.

We hurriedly found our way back to the truck without any samples, promising each other we would return. However, we ultimately decided environmental sleuthing was better left to someone else.

Back in the 1980s the paper mill knew the landfill would eventually reach capacity, so they were looking for creative ways to get rid of the sludge somewhere else. They found one answer during that decade in a statewide plan to spread the stuff on farmers' fields. A representative from the Natural Resources Council of Maine (NRCM) came to our town and, at a public meeting, supported the spreading of sludge on Maine farms. He extolled the use of it as a nitrogen-rich, natural fertilizer and a product that the paper mills in Maine would deliver to farmers for free.

We often brought our children to these meetings as an opportunity for learning. One of our sons, who was in college at the time, stood up and asked, "Are you serious about this endorsement?"

"Yes," the representative answered.

In a quiet and deliberate manner, the boy said, "Sir, you are an idiot."

Questions that were asked back in the eighties about sludge, and would continue to be asked some thirty-five years later, included "How long did you use it?" and "What did you do with the sludge that came from the waste?"

It seems we find it easier to recognize tragedy in hindsight rather than as it is happening. Sludge from paper mills was indeed used as fertilizer, but Maine farmers didn't know at the time that this sludge contained high concentrations of "forever chemicals," linked to many kinds of cancer and disease, and included dioxin, considered the most potent carcinogen known to man.

Numbers put things into perspective, and records compiled by the Maine Department of Environmental Protection (DEP) tell us eight paper companies were involved in the spreading of 500,000 cubic yards of paper mill waste in Maine from 1989 to 2016. It is probably a conservative and potentially incomplete figure that excludes the hundreds of thousands of cubic yards spread by wastewater-treatment plants, some of which process paper mill sludge. The Maine DEP was responsible for licensing and regulating the application of sludge. They sanctioned it, as did the NRCM, the governor, state and local governing boards, and the people themselves.

New legislation requires paper mills, as well as hundreds of other industrial facilities, to report the discharge of more than 120 types of polyfluoroalkyl substances (PFAS) and to file reports with the Toxics Release Inventory. Unfortunately, these reports only reflect current releases, not historic ones.

I often ask "what if" questions.

What if the leaders of our state, including governors and legislators, had paid attention to the science?

What if the many legislative leaders who came from these paper mill towns had been curious enough to set up an investigative panel to review the dangers of spreading contaminated sludge on the fields where our food is grown?

What if they had understood that paper mill sludge placed on top of the soil would eventually leach into the groundwater and contaminate our water supply?

What if they had recognized that the "unpleasant odors" in our town were actually not just unpleasant but extremely dangerous?

Thirty

The Meeting

O ur activist group waited months for a public meeting to occur where we could ask the Maine DEP why they would consider renewing and expanding an air emission permit for a paper mill that had already turned its immediate surroundings into a "sacrifice zone." Contaminated air caused significant deterioration to the health and quality of life of the residents of the Granite Bowl. Of this, there was no doubt. And yet, the DEP was fully prepared to let it continue, unchecked.

We were greeted at the door by a group of police officers in riot gear. Someone had alerted the police that a group of "dangerous environmental activists" were coming to the meeting. While it was true we could be described as defenders of the environment, it would be difficult to imagine that we could be called dangerous. We were all mothers, and we had no violent intentions.

The stage was set.

We walked, single file, into the Muskie Auditorium at Mountain Valley High School—a physician, a nurse, a neuro-scientist, a chemist, and a baker. DEP officials were seated at the front of the room around a long banquet table covered with flowing soft blue fabric. Everyone was given a bottle of water while upbeat flamenco music played in the background. We might have been arriving at a tropical resort, so positive and accommodating was the atmosphere.

A large screen covered most of the stage on which flashed images of a verdant, healthy river valley. There were no photos of the industrial mill complex, just blue skies and green grass. It was stunning. The photographer must have been lucky or waited patiently for a perfect day to take pictures, without particulate matter flying around like black pepper or an air inversion so thick everything was hidden in bonfire smoke.

The entire thing was stage-managed. It was meant to feel more like an afternoon of entertainment than a deadly serious meeting about the health of our families.

A young, attractive blonde woman walked confidently down the center aisle of the auditorium in three-inch heels and mounted the stairs to the stage. She walked to the podium, giving her hair a flirtatious toss. This woman had clearly been chosen to represent the pulp and paper industry to this audience. She was being used as a prop, and if she knew it, she didn't seem to mind one bit.

The woman smiled like she was about to open a Mary Kay convention.

"Hi, everyone," she said, looking somewhat confused that no one seemed to share her good mood. "I'm here to share with you the industrial position of environmental responsibility."

My friend Anne Morin, the neuroscientist, sat next to me. She leaned over and said, "I didn't know they had a position of environmental responsibility." Both by temperament and vocation, Anne was skeptical of the flashy misdirection on display at this meeting. She liked facts, not fluff.

For my part, I sat there picturing this young woman with a ponytail and pompoms. She could have easily been an R. J. Reynolds tobacco shill, except her shirt read MEADWESTVACO.

She continued her presentation, and it soon became clear to me that her intention was to avoid the topics we were there to discuss. She told us about her industry's good deeds and its ability to rescue people trapped on a mountainside with a highly trained and skilled rescue squad. She wanted everyone to know that this particular paper mill had been recognized for their rescue work by the governor himself. He was on their team.

And did we know and appreciate what the papermaking industry offered the community at large? In other words, did we understand how much money they contributed to the economy of the town? It was a veiled threat, a not-so-subtle reminder of the consequences for making trouble.

When she'd finished, the DEP presented an overview of their role in all of this. They said they tested for chloroform and nothing else, because that was all they could afford to do. Air emission testing was still in its infancy, and the state couldn't afford to do that either. They handed out a brochure with a high-minded, almost poetic mission statement. PROTECT THE PEOPLE, it said.

To me, these were just pretty words meant to distract from the truth. When it came to protecting, I believed the DEP used up all of its resources protecting industry. We were left to protect ourselves, if we could.

Although they knew the nature of the papermaking process, they claimed they couldn't tell us if the chemicals being dumped in our landfills and rivers and blown into our air were causing a high incidence of life-altering diseases, including functional disabilities, cancer, multiple sclerosis, asthma, Parkinson's disease, multiple myeloma, thyroid disease, diabetes, and on and on, a seemingly endless list of unnecessary suffering.

I thought about the bitter irony. Here we were, sitting in an auditorium named for Ed Muskie, the man who crafted the most meaningful environmental laws in the history of the country, and these people were just lying right to our faces, denying the dangers posed by the paper industry.

Ingrid, the physician among us, gave a PowerPoint presentation that showed black billowing smoke across the entire screen in a continuous loop. Ingrid's delivery was powerful. She presented a written list of questions and asked for answers.

But the DEP had no answers. Today was only for asking questions, they said, not for answering them. We the people wouldn't get any answers today. And, not to ruin any suspense, they would never actually get around to answering our questions.

The audience at large was invited to ask questions.

A group of students in the environmental studies program at Bates College stood up in unison. Ed Muskie had graduated from Bates and donated all of his papers and memorabilia to the school's archives. Bates has a highly respected environmental studies program, and the students asked probing questions. They clearly saw the big picture. Looking at the graphs presented by the DEP tracking the alarmingly high levels of chloroform in the valley, one of the students asked, "If I had lived in this area during those periods when high chloroform levels were registered, what would the effects have been on my development and general health?"

"It wouldn't have been good," said the DEP officer.

Next, Tim Gallant's twelve-year-old daughter, Mary, rose to address the room. Tim had called me the day before the hearing, wanting to know if I thought it would be okay for Mary to speak. Tim was a local boy who had become a police officer in town. His wife had severe asthma and was being treated for problems relating to that illness. Mary had her own health problems and had recently undergone surgery. Tim blamed her illness, as well as his wife's asthma, on emissions from the mill. He could sit on his deck and hit the gigantic wood-chip pile across the street with a rock. He wanted out but wasn't hopeful he would find anyone to buy his property. It had already been on the market for three years.

Tim called the DEP every week; they knew him on a first-name basis. He had a video camera pointed at the stacks and filmed whenever he thought the mill was exceeding emission limits. He believed they doubled the emissions at night because it was harder for people to see what was happening.

We could tell, and we reported, but nothing was done about any of it.

When Tim called the DEP, he got the runaround. The DEP referred him to the Department of Health and Human Services. There, his calls got bounced from one office to another. Tim never got any answers or solutions, just spent a lot of time on hold. He kept a list of new cancers diagnosed in town. On this particular day, his list included: Wendy, age forty-five, ovarian cancer; Gloria, age forty-five, ovarian cancer; Eugene, prostate cancer; Paul, prostate cancer; Gerald, multiple myeloma; and Robert, lung cancer.

In her delicate twelve-year-old voice, Mary asked what effect all the other chemicals—that weren't tested or even reported—could have on the quality of her life. The windows of the house she shares with her parents were splattered with mill debris that looked and smelled like pitch. It was sticky and hard to wash off.

She had to cover her ears at certain times of the day when the noise was so loud and violent that she couldn't tolerate it. She had to breathe the air and live the lie. She was a young girl that the DEP was supposed to protect. She didn't need to be rescued from a mountaintop; she was trapped in her own home.

After Mary finished, Ingrid stood again to ask for a listing of all the mill's emission points. She wanted to let the mill know we knew they may have been in compliance for some of the burning stacks but they owned others that were not.

"What about the other emission points not reported to the DEP?" Ingrid asked. "What about those pollutants? How are they handled?"

An industrial engineer representing the mill said there were other emission points, such as bathroom vents, that were not being monitored. He managed to keep a straight face as he said this.

Bathroom vents?

They were mocking us!

Ingrid gave up.

Her husband, John, asked the next—and perhaps most damning—question.

"Do the executives from this mill live in the valley?"

Heads turned at the table, but no one answered. They simply ignored his question.

The paper mill encouraged fifty of its workers to attend the meeting and show support. They sat there, silent, in what seemed like an attempt to intimidate us.

Only one stood to speak. He said he worked at the plant and lived in the Granite Bowl, adding he was "proud" to raise his family here.

But being proud has nothing to do with an air emission permit. It was yet another diversion and a way to use loyalty as a lever with the workers.

I spoke that night about some of my own experiences as a nurse. The effect chemicals had on my patients. The nausea, chest pain, burning eyes, and muscle aches that were our daily bread. The cancers, of course, and the other diseases linked to the various chemicals the mill put out.

The audience of millworkers stared straight ahead as I spoke. Nothing was said after I'd finished.

In the end, it was all for show.

The DEP failed to live up to their fancy mission statement.

After the meeting, our group of five women continued to speak truth to power despite the intimidation, the denial, the willful ignorance, the outright lies.

As for the pulp and paper industry, they would spend money to rescue people who climb mountains and get lost, but they will do nothing to address the health issues of Cancer Valley. More people will die, painfully and needlessly and often far too young.

In 1991 an ABC affiliate came to Rumford and produced a segment called "Cancer Valley," focusing on the cancer rates in our town. It was televised in Boston, but never aired in Maine. Lawsuits were threatened. This segment became a cult film shown to students studying the impact of pollution on small communities. In the segment, Doc performs a bedside call to a boyhood friend who worked at the mill and was dying of cancer.

In a follow-up segment filmed a decade later, it is Doc who is dying of cancer. Given everything he has seen and heard, Doc is asked if he thinks any changes will be made at the mill.

"No." he says.

Epilogue

Writers write for many reasons. I wanted to write my story, but where I started is not where I ended. The act of writing allowed me to better understand the details of my life that played out in both darkness and light; in private and in public. Looking back, it seems three of the biggest influences on my life—the Catholic Church, my husband, and the Rumford paper mill—all presented two different faces: a caring public one and a problematic private one.

The issues of the Catholic Church are complicated and that story is better told elsewhere, but its attempt to control me and keep me compliant played a key role in the decisions of my adult life. The Rumford paper mill, including the powerful people behind it, was a kind, benevolent force that built the town and tried to care for its citizens. It also dumped toxins into the river and into the air, creating disastrous pollution and, I believe, essentially killing many of the very people it sought to protect.

And finally my husband, Edward "Doc" Martin was a compassionate family doctor, beloved by his patients, and a selfless, tireless crusader for justice, particularly against the sins of the paper mill. He was also a verbally abusive and controlling man who delivered withering criticisms to keep me down, not to mention his serial infidelity.

Finding my voice after all this was a challenge and this book, *And Poison Fell from the Sky*, was not only a cathartic exercise, but an important step in finding peace.

Why write about all this now? I was asked by some. *It's history.* Yes, it is a story of the past, but it echoes in the present and the future. The legacy pollutants the paper mill has left behind for decades will have a great effect on our future. While no one has officially tied toxins from the mill to the sky-high cancer rate in Cancer Valley, it is an undeniable fact that the Androscoggin River, like other rivers in Maine, is polluted with legacy chemicals. Once sources of nature's bounty, our rivers flow listless, carrying toxins to the sea and polluting communities along the way. It seems only common sense that the chemicals have caused, and will continue to cause, health problems. Some of the legacy pollutants do not degrade; instead they bioaccumulate in our food chain. Some are too heavy to flow, so they remain in place, effectively polluting forever. This is the legacy we must finally confront and acknowledge. This is the sin of the father, and it is up to the children to deal with it.

As for Doc, I both loved him and hated him. I still do. Emotionally, it was not easy to relive those days in great detail, but it was important. By recounting my life on paper, I could see again those days and nights spent in fear of his brutal criticism. I could better understand the methods he used to control me. He was unpredictable. He could be both loving and abusive in the same moment. I feared him, yet I needed him at the same time. I needed him for the safety of my children, their lives and expectations, their future. I could not forego that for my comfort. In my mind, leaving him was not a realistic option. Once he was diagnosed with cancer, it was an impossibility. It may have been because of the values instilled in me by the Sisters of Mercy at Mercy Hospital School of Nursing in Portland, but here was a sick man who needed my help. I would learn to live with his manipulation, his insults, threats, and isolation to keep to the status quo and stick to my nursing values. I would cling to moments of less pain, making myself believe a change in his behavior would come.

It didn't come without great cost.

Doc's moods swung wildly between being loving and abusive. Fear was as big a part of our relationship as love. I feared what he would do and how he would do it. As a result, I lost the ability to define and even believe my own reality, my interpretation of things, my point of view.

Doc was altruistic, fighting for the underdog, the innocent. He fought injustice in the world even while perpetrating it in our home. He focused on the air we breathed and the water we drank, but he neglected the brutal emotional environment he forced his family to live in. I think in chasing the truth about pollution, Doc lost sight of the truth about himself.

In his waning days, Doc never stopped telling me I should die with him. It was scary, but in the end, when it was most important, I found a way to break free. I survived.

My children also survived. They were able to successfully navigate the emotional minefields of a large and dysfunctional family, a fact that speaks to their individual courage and strength. After high school, they left the valley to follow careers in medicine, music, and business. I have been able to enjoy the successes of my children, and I've watched my grandchildren grow with ideas and dreams of their own.

As for me, I methodically rebuilt my self-confidence. After Doc died, I still needed to earn a living. I resumed my career as a nurse and continued to work as an environmental activist. I further explored my interest in music and moved to the small resort town of Rangeley. It was there that I truly found my voice.

In this small community, nestled in the mountains of Maine, I discovered a peace that had eluded me for my entire life. I joined a writers' group where I shared the trust and talents of others who write for many of the same reasons I do. I opened a small antique shop called Dallas Hill Antiques and enjoyed the social camaraderie that goes along with the business of preserving history. I continued my music studies, learning the nuances of the church organ through study with the minister of music at the Church of the Good Shepherd. I taught piano to aspiring young musicians for nearly ten years and helped create a platform for women to express their own talents as singers, dancers, and actors in an annual revue called The Diva Show. I am thrilled that the show continues today.

It is safe to say, it has been quite a life. My life. My story.

Acknowledgments

I first thank my children, their spouses, my family, and my friends, who with kindness and loving understanding supported me throughout this process.

With gratitude, I offer thanks to writers' groups found locally and afar who encourage writers to write. Special thanks to the Kingston New York Public Library Writers' Group (including Leigh Ryan) and to the Rumford Writers' Group.

Thanks to my editors, who reviewed this manuscript with professional wisdom and to Islandport Press and its staff for turning pages into print. Thanks to Kerri Arsenault for her courageous portrayal of life in *Mill Town* and for daring to go there.

I am grateful to those of you who listened and read (especially Kayce Waters).

About the Author

MarieThérèse (Terry) Martin is a registered nurse, originally from Rumford, Maine. She experienced a life clouded by toxic emissions and saw the effects of the papermill industry on her community firsthand. As a main character in Kerri Arsenault's 2020 bestseller, *Mill Town*, Martin was instrumental in the exploration of the area's toxins and disease, providing primary-source documents and stimulating conversations. Martin is the author of *Le Visage de ma Grandmère*, a mixed-genre look at Acadian history and cuisine. She co-founded the Acadian Historical Society and an annual Fiddle Contest, featuring Acadian culture, cuisine, and music, in the Rumford-Mexico area as a nod to her heritage. She has three children and several grandchildren. She now lives in Hartford.